gaz regan's
**Annual Manual
for Bartenders**
2013

gaz regan's
Annual Manual
for Bartenders
2013

gaz regan

Mixellany Limited

Copyright © 2013 Gary Regan

All rights reserved. Printed in the United Kingdom. No part of this book may be used or reproduced in any manner whatsoever without written permission except in the case of brief quotations embodied in critical articles and reviews. For information address Mixellany Limited, 3 Eyford Cottages, Upper Slaughter, Cheltenham, Gloucestershire GL54 2JL United Kingdom..

Mixellany books may be purchased for educational, business, or sales promotional use. For information, please write to Mixellany Limited, 3 Eyford Cottages, Upper Slaughter, Cheltenham, Gloucestershire GL54 2JL United Kingdom. or email jared@mixellany.com

First edition

ISBN 13: 978-1-907434-40-2

British Library Cataloguing in Publication Data.

A catalogue record for this book is available from the British Library.

This book is dedicated to
Henry Ernest Bryden Besant, 1972 – 2013.
Save a barstool for me up there, please, Henry.
And if you could have a Negroni waiting. . . .

Acknowledgements

Thanks, as always, to the Divine Ms. M., aka Martha Schueneman, my trusty editor who makes putting these annual manuals out almost painless, and also to Jared Brown and Anistatia Miller for being great publishers, and damned good friends.

And this year I have to shout out a huge thanks to everyone who contributed to this edition. You'll see their names as you go through the book. Not one of these people were paid a dime for their time or their expertise, but in the spirit of the bartender, they just gave me what I needed in order to make this book represent the global bar scene in 2013.

Huge thanks to one and all.

By the Same Author

gaz regan's Annual Manual for Bartenders 2012
gaz regan's Annual Manual for Bartenders 2011
gaz regan's 101 Best New Cocktails
The Cocktailian Chronicles: Life with the Professor
The Book of Bourbon & Other Fine American Whiskies

Table of Contents

Introduction
Part 1
    Bartenders Changing the World   **11**

Chapter 1
    The Mindful Bartender   12

Chapter 2
    How to Become a Better Bartender   31

Chapter 3
    Barbacks: The Unsung Heroes of the Craft   40

Chapter 4
    Bartenders' Most Embarrassing Moments   51

Chapter 5
    Ladies Who Lush
        by Francine Cohen   66

Chapter 6
    Nothing Like a Dame   73

Chapter 7
    Best Blogs of the Year   138

Chapter 8
    The Gazzers   148

Part 2
  Bar Geekery — 171

Chapter 9
  A Tale of Longing and Fulfillment
    by Tomas Estes — 172

Chapter 10
  The Most Interesting Man in the World
    by Philip Greene — 175

Chapter 11
  Ingredient Focus: Lillet — 180

Chapter 12
  Ingredient Focus: Ice
    by Richard Boccato — 192

Chapter 13
  Ingredients Focus: Bitters
    by Jamie Boudreau — 204

Chapter 14
  Ingredient Focus: Extreme Aperol
    and the No Baloney Negroni
    by Camper English — 212

Index — 215

About the Author — 219

Introduction

This, I believe, is the Year of the Woman Bartender, and although plenty of men are mentioned in this edition, you'll notice that I've really concentrated heavily on the women in this year's *Manual*. Why? Because they deserve it.

Tending bar is a male-dominated craft no matter how you look at it, but for the past couple of years, female bartenders have been growing in number, and more than a few women behind the stick have been doing things that make me sit up and take notice. Speed Rack springs to mind, and there are many more women-instigated happenings in the bar world that deserve a big shout out.

That's it from me, then (though I'll be adding many comments throughout this book). Hope you enjoy the third edition of the *Annual Manual for Bartenders*.

gaz regan

gaz regan's ANNUAL MANUAL FOR BARTENDERS

Part 1

Bartenders Changing the World

Bartenders can, and do, change this world in so many ways. They donate to charities, work in soup kitchens, and they help their guests by not only making them happy, but also by jumping in where and when they are needed, no matter what the task. Keep up the good work, my friends, you make my little heart glad.

Chapter 1

The Mindful Bartender

As you'll see in this chapter, the mindful concept is growing in leaps and bounds within the international bartender community. This, as you might imagine, makes my little heart glad, since I believe that mindfulness is the heart of the bartender's craft.

As I tread this Earth day by day, I'm reminded on a regular basis that I need to keep re-reading books that show me the right way to live in order to be happy, and in order to try to show others how to be happy, too. I remember years ago when I was at a family gathering, and my brother-in-law, a Christian priest, had his Bible with him. "Haven't you finished that book yet?" I asked him. And we both had a good laugh at that one.

Now, though, I find myself listening to audiobooks on mindfulness over and over again. Fact is that if we don't keep reminding ourselves of this stuff, our egos seize the opportunity to take control of our lives, and we get lost in the dream again.

Before I launch into this chapter, then, let me share with you the titles of some of the books I've read and re-read over the years, along with a few short comments about each one.

You might find some of these books to be of interest as you walk the path of the bartender.

Books to Consider on Your Path to Mindful Bartending

I started my journey into mindfulness by reading **Deepak Chopra**. He's good at tying together science and spirituality, so his stuff is easy to digest. *The Spontaneous Fulfillment of Desire: Harnessing the Infinite Power of Coincidence* is one of my faves by Deepak, but you can just choose any of his stuff that you feel drawn toward.

Another Chopra book that has served me well is *Creating Affluence*. This one not only reminds you that affluence isn't always about money, but it also offers great advice on how to be successful in your professional life.

Then there's **Eckhart Tolle**, another fave. German guy with a squeaky voice. He's pretty amusing. Both *The Power of Now* and *A New Earth* are extraordinary.

And of course there's the *Bhagavad Gita*. Here's a short-ish description of this epic that I've taken from Bhagavad-Gita.org:

> The Bhagavad-Gita is considered by eastern and western scholars alike to be among the greatest spiritual books the world has ever known. In a very clear and wonderful way the Supreme Lord Krishna describes the science of self-realization and the exact process by which a human being can establish their eternal relationship with God. In terms of pure, spiritual knowledge the Bhagavad-Gita is incomparable. Its intrinsic beauty is that its knowledge applies to all human beings and does not postulate any sectarian ideology or secular view. It is approachable from the sanctified realms of all religions and is glorified as the epitome of all spiritual teachings.

This book is a slog, but it's also one of those books that you'll probably end up reading one day. The easiest translation

I've found is *The Bhagavad Gita: A New Translation* by Stephen Mitchell. Check it out if you're ready to tackle this one.

And if you want to hold off reading the Gita for a while, you might want to invest in this collection of audio-recordings of lectures that Ram Dass gave at the Naropa University in Boulder, Colorado, in the 1970s: *Love, Service, Devotion, and the Ultimate Surrender: Ram Dass on the Bhagavad Gita*. **Ram Dass**—born Richard Alpern—is probably best described as being an old hippie. He used to teach at Harvard until they kicked him out in 1963, and he then went to India, trained under a guru, and became a spiritual leader in his own right. What I love most of all about Ram Dass is the fact that he has a great sense of humor, and he doesn't take himself too seriously. Listening to his audio collection, for me at least, is akin to hanging with a guy who knows what life's all about, and knows how to crack wise about it, too. And no matter what age you are right now, Ram Dass is relevant to you. Trust me on this.

Rivals and Competition: A Mindful Approach

Earlier editions of the *Annual Manual* have focused on certain aspects of and challenges to mindfulness. This year, the main subject I'd like to address is how to deal with your rivals in business. What do you do if you open a bartender consultancy business and someone else—maybe even someone you considered a friend—opens a very similar enterprise right next door? Or suppose the boss hires a new bartender and your regulars just love him or her to bits, and you start thinking that you're losing your popularity?

How do you fight back in these situations?

It's pretty easy: You don't fight. It may seem counterintuitive, but I've found that the best way to deal with rivals and, strange as this may seem, to actually maximize my business, has been to help promote *their* businesses. It pays off in spades—really! Here are a few guidelines:

1. Make sure that you think highly of your competitor. If that's not the case, then it's probably best that you just step back, don't say anything bad about them, and let nature run its course.
2. If you do think highly of them, tell the world about it. Promote them at any given opportunity.
3. The secret to this is to promote them by truly wishing them the very best in terms of success. If you're faking it, this will not work for you.
4. Don't ever stop helping to promote your competitors.
5. Now all you have to do is sit back and watch your business take off. This is the way in which the universe works. Put true positive vibes out there, and you shall be rewarded. Promise.
6. And then watch for a bonus: As your competitors realize that you have sincerely good intentions, they will be behind you all the way.

There are more ways of supporting your competitors than just saying good things about them. You can actually give them work. If you are a consultant, for instance, I'm betting that there are one or two aspects of the business that you can deal with, but perhaps they aren't your strong suits, right? That's true for just about anyone.

Do you know a competitor who handles these weaknesses of yours brilliantly? You have a choice: You can do a so-so job on something you might not particularly enjoy, or you can bring your competition to the table. Tell your client that you can design a fabulous new cocktail list that will be very profitable, you can train their bartenders on all sorts of fronts, but if they really want to re-design their bar stations, you'll have to bring in a friend of yours who does a far better job than you could ever do.

That's my mindful focus for this year, guys. Hope this plan work for you as well as it's worked for me. I've never looked back since I started taking this approach to business. Now I'm turning this chapter over to other bartenders who are walking the path of mindfulness. As you'll see, there are many paths you can take.

Mindful Quotes of the Year

Here's a selection of my favorite quotes from bartenders this year. Pretty inspirational they are! (In order to meet deadlines I have to stop adding stuff sometime in November, so the first quote you're seeing in this edition dates from November, 2011. It's a doozy, though.)

I'll Do My Best to Show You a Good Time

"Thanksgiving Eve is usually a very busy night filled with friends and families reuniting in the city, and the bars have a totally different vibe than usual. Most people have just taken off from work for a long weekend so it's almost like a winter break for elementary school students. A lot of the time guests' behavior reflects the 'school's-out' ethos. Sure it can be stressful, but we're in a stressful business. As a bartender and businessman, I would be a fool to complain about how crowded my bar is on a Wednesday night. Open the doors, come on in, and I'll do my best to show you a good time. With the proper mindset and precautions, the so called 'amateur' night doesn't have to be amateur."

Steve Schneider, Principal Bartender at **Employees Only**, New York City. Source: Eat.com, Wednesday, November 23, 2011, by Leslie Pariseau.

gaz sez: *This is a classic case of being able to accept things as they are, something that lies in the heart of Zen philosophy. We are in a stressful business, as Steve says, and the busier the bar gets, the more stressful our jobs become. And the bigger our tip-cups get. Approach these nights with the right attitude and "amateur nights" can become a win-win situation for all involved.*

A Profession Built on a Foundation of Hospitality

Some of the most amazing cocktail creators I've ever seen have been shitty bartenders. Many of them have encyclopedic knowledge of drink recipes, history, spirits, beer, wine, etc. But they never learned hospitality; they never learned to serve. I take great pride in being a barman. It is a profession built on a foundation of hospitality. Many, many before me and many of my peers also take great pride in serving and pleasing people.

Sean Kenyon, Williams and Graham, Denver, CO. Source: Denver Westward Blogs.

The Girl at the End of the Bar

Are you a mixologist or a bartender?

"Honestly, I'm not sure I know how to answer because, ultimately, I'm just a bartender. We are drink-slingers. Showmen, therapists, short-time friends and shot-buddies. We break up fights for a living and wash dishes. The big questions of the world are answered by those fancier than us, but if we have time, and if she's amenable, we might introduce you to the girl who's sitting at the end of the bar."

Michael Neff, New York. Source: Zagat.com.

Able to Relate

What do you hate about [tending bar]?

"I don't know if there is anything I necessarily hate. There are definitely times you feel tested or tried by the process, but I think the most challenging thing is to be able not just to serve a fabulous product, but to be able to relate to people at the same time. Obviously they're both really important, but to be able to maintain that high level for eight, nine, 10 hours of service so that the 150th person has the same experience as the first person—that's definitely the most challenging part."

Tommie Cheng, Cocktail Bar, Toronto, Canada. Source: Blogto.com.

You're Here to Serve People

What's the most important trait for a bartender to have?

"Being humble is important in being a bartender. It's a simple thing, not a question of skill; it's a question of character. Anyone can, literally, in a ten-minute lesson, make a martini as good as me or anyone else. But how many people will go to work for eight hours and every single martini they make is made as good as they can make it? That's a rare person. You reach into the freezer, and the glass that you are touching is not exactly cold, and your back hurts. Will you reach that much further to reach the glass that has been in the freezer longer and is cold? No amount of skill or knowledge will replace character. Bartending is a service position, you're here to serve people. You put your ego aside for eight hours, and make other people's interests more important than yours, and it is a wonderful thing, it's a freeing thing. I find it far more interesting than distilling whiskey. Bartending is simpler and easier than other things, but it is more rewarding. It's what I want to do."

Sasha Petraske, New York. Source: sacurrent.com (San Antonio).

Positive Interaction

"I personally find the hardest thing to do is to consistently have a positive attitude. I pride myself on always offering a smile and giving someone a quality interaction when I deal with them across the bar. We all have our up and down days, so giving someone a smile even when you're not feeling like it is an art. Almost anyone can remember drink recipes, but not everyone can consistently create a positive interaction with their guest."

Tim Cooper, New York. Source: behindtheburner.com.

gaz sez: I first met Tim in 2012 when he won a TV bartender competition organized by AKA Wine Geek. His challenge was to deal with 20+ unruly customers, myself included, all of whom needed drinks, and all of whom had strange or awkward requests. He handled it beautifully.

Give Customers What They Want

"I think there's a tendency now for bartenders to make drinks for bartenders. I'm hoping that's a phase. It's a sign of a growing confidence in bartenders, but not enough confidence to be simple again. And give customers what they want."

Nick Strangeway, Strangehill, London. Source: FoodRepublic.com.

It's All About Giving Someone What They Want

"[At the Brooklyn bar] we were taught to build cocktails with our heart in place, to close our eyes and visualize ourselves as being content. And when we make a drink we remember that it's a privilege to do what we do and that not everybody gets a chance to do that in our life. Anybody can mix a drink; a robot can mix a drink. But to actually have feelings when you produce that and put it into a glass and have somebody enjoy a piece of something that you created—few bartenders have that opportunity. At the end of the day, it's all about giving someone what they want. They come there to see you. You invite them into your home. The bar scene can be a very scary place when it's not done with love."

Anonymous. Source: BusinessInsider.com.

Be that Blessing for Someone Today

"Good morning sweet 's!!! Allow God to share peace within your heart as you start your day! Your attitude can affect someone's life just as much as your attitude can be a blessing!! Take the step and be that blessing for someone today xoxo!!!"

Elba Girón, Brand Activation Manager, **Edrington Group.** Source: Facebook posting.

Mindful eMails

Throughout the course of the year I get various emails on the subject of mindfulness behind the bar, and some of them are pretty inspiring. I'm sharing a few of these emails with you here, hoping that they might help you understand how well mindfulness fits into all aspects of our lives as bartenders.

Michael Joseph Helgeson, Bartender, Tampa Bay Brewing Company, Ybor City, Tampa, FL

My dear Mr. Regan:

Like any other night, I get home after tending the bar; tired, sipping on a beverage finally served up to and for myself, going about the routine acts of leisure in my more than humble apartment. I do some dishes, put on some music. I open the computer, no real intention behind the motion, just routine. Facebook absorbs another 15 minutes of my life. Fruitless but not unpleasant. And then, as per usual, I check my email. A small sea of automated messages pretending to be my very best of friends saturates an inbox that I long to be full of sincere and meaningful communication. Alas. But what's this I see? Something familiar! It is the title of the first chapter of a book I once read, loved, was inspired by, and then put aside, like so many books before it. And where is this cool and refreshing reminder of a mindfulness that promises to enrich ANY act of life with meaning, joy, and purpose come from??? Gaz Regan. Well I'll be damned.

So, Mr. Regan, this email is a simple thank you. The bar, like life, has been both kind and harsh to me. Ebb and Flow. But your newsletter came as a gentle reminder that regardless of all the peripherals, the bar is an opportunity, a stage on which to ply the fundamental trade of being a genuine human person. It is a trade that ought to be practiced everywhere, anywhere, and with reckless abandon. And the word is a beautiful place to start. I guess it's time I got back to it.

Reinhard Pohorec, Bartender,
The Sign Cocktail Bar, Vienna, Austria

For a couple of weeks, the *Annual Manual* 2012 has been lying on my night table, alongside all the whisky and spirits books I've been eager to devour!

After a very long and laborious shift, probably around 5 o'clock in the morning, something really "forced" me to open the *Manual* and start reading, although I was so tired and waiting for the quiet sleep to come over me!

It was the first time when I came across the idea of Gaz' "mindful bartending", I was so drawn in to the lines I read, deeply touched and so happy, I simply couldn't stop making my way through the pages. And I realized: that's just what I've been experiencing and feeling over the last couple of months, all the love, all the passion.

I like to talk about the last two years of my life as "a spirits journey," I was honored and pleased to meet and work with so many fantastic people, coming across some amazing products and feeling such a deep love and happiness for what I'm doing.

The pages I read in the Manual kept me awake that night and I sat down in front of my laptop and said to myself: I just have to write to Mr Regan, telling him a bit of what I've experienced and letting him know just how inspiring he's been for my journey, even though I've never had the chance to meet him in person or to talk to him before.

Being well assured that you, Gaz, and your amazing "helping hands" have to work yourselves through thousands of e-mails, it became a heart's desire to write you these lines, not because I want to tell you just what an amazing bartender I think I am, or trying to advertise myself... It is more like a prayer for me and a silent thank you - to you as a person - and in a general sense, being just a humble and thankful man at the age of 24, telling you a little about my "spirits journey"!

At this very young age many people do not worry all too much about everyday problems, life in general, the future or even about tomorrow. It's all about fun, the other sex, drinking alcohol for purpose, parties and nights out, but for me life has never been the easy way and I had to climb a few hills (sometimes mountains). Always having "learned" to do things as correctly and as perfectly as possible isn't a bad thing at all but it can build up a huge wall of pressure and whenever I had to think about my future plans, everything about education, job and career for me was stress, fear, sorrow and other people's over-expectation.

A crucial illness stopped all my plans and forced me to slow down my ambitions and my economic studies, which I'd had started because I thought it to be a safe choice and career option. I had no power left, my body got to an absolute limit, I didn't know where to go or what to do, and I had to learn what it feels like to be on a very fine line between life and death.

At least there was a little spark of hope and energy in me, telling me that I needed something enjoyable, something that I'd do because I wanted to and not because I thought I had to, something touchable, real. Maybe that's why I have such a deep love and respect for people's hard work, labour, traditional handcrafted things, agriculture, ... But it was certainly my appreciation and sensitivity for aromas and taste, food and cooking that led me to the Wine & Spirit Education Trust (WSET). I didn't know the difference between Chardonnay and Riesling, or that something like Chardonnay even existed, but I was open-minded, eager to smell and taste, learn and in a few months I devoured as many books as I could get hold of, went to tastings and met amazing new people.

Well, in short, I had to face a deadly disease, make cruel and crucial experiences and learn things about life. I'm absolutely not proud of it, but I think everything in life happens for a certain reason and fighting through can either break you or make you stronger, telling and teaching you something. Everything is part of my history, I have to accept it, treasure it, because it led me to the here and now, and if I can be happy with what I am today, all in all, it was a good way!!

WSET especially brought me to spirits and fortified wines, gave me an amazing tasting experience and awareness and incidentally I also wanted to take the courses at the First Austrian Barkeeper School.

Looking back, I can't believe what happened ever since, I found home, I met so many fantastic people (grand seigneurs like Erich Wassicek accepted me into the Vienna Bar Community, he actually regarded me as kind of a son, a colleague, a friend, a professional), I had the honor to fly over to the Berlin Bar Convent (BCB) last year and be part of Gaz' gin tasting, winning the city award with the VBC, and my barchef and good friend Kan Zuo (The Sign) asked me whether I could imagine becoming bartender alongside him! (one the most important steps along the bartending way).

i had the amazing chance to be part of the World Class 2012 Western Europe finals after winning GSA, and I was nominated "newcomer of the year" for this year's mixology awards in Berlin. I can work with amazing products but, and that's the most important aspect of all, I also learned and understood that I'm not primarily serving drinks, I'm serving guests!

Some of your books, Gaz, accompanied me along the way, as I said, it was my great pleasure to participate in one of your tastings but it wasn't until a few weeks ago when I received the 2012 *Annual Manual*. When I reached for the book ('though it was about 6am) and started reading, it's hard for me to describe what happened to me, I was touched, I got emotional which, after working 12 hours, being completely tired, actually just wanting to get some sleep was quite surprising or unexpected. the book was really speaking to me, telling me "hey, that's just everything you experienced over the last year. (Additionally I had a very hard time and struggle with a close family member .... hmm, well, it was my dad to be honest .... "anger and forgiveness" spoke to me at that very moment, just right in time, perfect match! suddenly I felt the power and energy, and the love to make a first step towards him and solving a couple of issues.)

Whilst hitting rock bottom and being devastated, I often asked my mom: I don't know what to do, where to go, what's my way, my place in life, ... and she always responded: don't try to plan everything, do not always look too far, just walk, and your way will unfold whilst being on the road. It was so damned hard and took me so long, but now I can understand what she meant.

I am so thankful for all the people around me, for having found my true love and passion, having the chance to live this passion, sharing it with fantastic friends, colleagues, guests and friends and working with them, plus all the amazing products we have at hand. All that is my motivation, it is a heart's desire and my great pleasure, always staying thankful, being a humble servant and epicure...

Thank you, to who or what ever might be out there, some might call it god, others fate, karma, chakra, whatever... thanks to you, mr regan, for being a "mentor" and a great example, for somehow also sending me the right words just in the right moment!

It would be my pleasure one day shaking your hand and personally telling you just how thankful, impressed and touched I am, probably with a great drink in the other hand!

cheers to you, god bless you, all my sincere wishes and best spirits,

yours, Reini (Reinhard Pohorec, Vienna)

Yael Amyra, brand ambassador
Purity Vodka and **Wemyss Malts**,
plus columnist for **Drink Me Magazine**,
San Francisco, CA

Good morning!

I enjoyed your piece which reminded me about finding moments to forgive those who are offended by me or I've offended (angered). These often-fleeting moments when unaddressed, altogether become buried in my day to day busy-ness. But my [brain] tends to percolate these moments of truth back into my subconscious, attempting to remind me that much inner work needs attending to like a garden needs water and nutrients to bloom.

How does that apply to me when I'm behind the bar . . . ? When a patron feels that my cocktails or speed of delivery or attentiveness to service details fall short of their expectations. "Can't they see I'm in the weeds, five deep and slinging fabulous drinks solo; or don't they know that a fine cocktail takes time to craft? How dare they glare at me, short tip me or be condescending!?!?" I used to say whether I was in the weeds or holding court over my regulars? Truth is I miss these fleeting lucid moments of being behind the bar as a "moving-walking-sprinting" meditation practice. It's when my regulars or new bar patrons saw me with my most authentic self: being in service and helping them feel good or better for their visit at the bar. Perceived "slights" from my patrons and the simple zen of bringing together delightful drinks to lift up the "little daily sufferings" as an offering to soothe the misunderstood yearnings is a gift. I miss these intense moments when my mindfulness-meta practice are right there, front and center for about six to eight intense hours off really being in the presence of practicing forgiveness and loving kindness in front and behind the bar.

Thanks for the opportunity for me to time-travel here, just so I can come back to the breath and the truth behind why I love(d) bartending and those ornery folks I serve(d).

Yael Amyra

Chapter 2

How to Become a Better Bartender

Last year I received an email from a bartender named David Herpin asking how he could improve his skills. Here's what he wrote:

> You don't know who I am, but I am a bartender, I admire your status within the industry and I ask only for your advice on how to become a better bartender and progress myself in the industry such as you have. Any resources, advice, or guidance would be so helpful to me and my career, thank you. (For the record, David works at Galatoire's and Maison Bourbon in New Orleans.)

I try to answer all emails that come my way, unless they're telling me that I just won $17,000,000 in the Ecuadorean National Lottery, of course, so I dashed off a paragraph of what I thought was fairly decent advice:

> The best advice I can offer, I think, is that you pick working bartenders who you admire, and go watch them work, and ask them questions. Most bartenders are fairly open to talking about how they do what they do.

The following day I got an email from Dale DeGroff, who wrote to tell me that he'd received the same email from David. Here's how Dale answered the letter:

> I can only say that I was swept away by the life in the bars of New York City and I wanted to be part of it. I worked in bars and restaurants, paying attention and learning along the way. Sometimes from mentors who were also passionate about the life in the Bar and Grill ... sometimes from the employees I worked alongside. Just be open to growing your skills and find that where ever you can, the dishwasher can teach you things about the business that the owner may never know. If you feel this passion to be a part of that world and you act on it you will always have fulfillment in your life and that is success.

Yes, Dale put more thought into his reply than I. What can I say? I was pretty busy that day, and my cat was sick, and I was on deadline, and I had a yoga class, and. . . .

Anyway, these emails led me to thinking about asking a number of other successful industry professionals to jot down a paragraph or two on this subject.

We all have different experiences that have influenced us, so we all bring something different to the table. You're about to read the responses I received.

Before that, though, I'd like to ask each and every bar professional who reads this to think about *your* best advice for new bartenders. Or what advice did you get when you started out that made a difference to your career? I'll use the best in an upcoming project or two. Please write to me at gaz@ardentspirits.com, and don't forget to tell me your full name, your position, the name of the bar where you work, and tell me which city it's in, too, please. Ta Muchly!

Dan Warner, Global On Premise Specialist, Absolut Vodka.

Treat every customer as good as you would if they were your future father-in-law sitting at the bar.

Give them the most hospitable service you can muster, serve the best drink you can. Don't overdo it or be sycophantic, just remember that person is important to you and to other people.

Everything else should come easy.

Jared Brown, Director, **Mixellany Limited** plus Master Distiller, **Sipsmith Distillery**, London, UK.

Years ago I was terrified of speaking in public. So when I had no choice but to make a major presentation I asked Tad Hayashi, then a VP with Japan Airlines and one of the most natural speakers I'd seen, how he did it. His advice may have been about public speaking, but it applies equally, as I later discovered, to bartending.

Tad said, "Before you step up to the podium find a place where you can be alone for a moment. Go anyplace where no one can see you. Step into a closet. Head to the toilet and lock yourself in a stall. Then, once you're there, look down and make absolutely sure your fly is zipped up."

I still think of that whenever I'm stepping up on stage or behind the bar (which is really the same thing). I still follow his instructions, and it never fails to put a smile on my face. And it is that smile, as much as the securely zipped fly, that starts every shift off on a positive note and sets the tone for the duration.

Lynn House, Chief Mixologist, **Blackbird**, Chicago, IL.

How does one become a better bartender? The first question I raise is why is one a bartender at all? Is it because no one else would hire you, is it because you consider yourself something else and you are just paying the bills, or is it because you love it?

No matter what you choose to do in life, you will spend the majority of your waking hours at your job, so you had better love it. If love for the craft, passion for what you do and willingness to learn are the crux of what defines you as a bartender, then you already have an amazing foundation.

I know bartenders who have amazing people skills—but know jack about what is on their back bar, I know bartenders who have an amazing wealth of knowledge but have zero people skills. Being the best that you can is learning how to marry the two. Remember at the end of the day, despite all the celebrity and hype that is happening in this industry, you are in the hospitality business. Sounds simple, but so many of today's younger 'tenders seem to forget.

So get over the attitude. When a guest walks into your bar, know it's not they who are the privileged ones, it's you. You are the best friend, the lawyer, the doctor, the psychiatrist... etc. Too many bartenders act like the guest should be in awe of them, when it is you who should be in awe of your guest—after all, it is they who pay the bills.

Second, if you are in this business to become famous, well then your success will be only temporary. Why? Because at the end of the day BS always shines through. You should be behind the stick because you love it, because it is your passion—this cannot be taught. It's either in you or it's not. Some of my favorite bartenders in the world have done nothing more than pour me a draft—but their joy shone through.

Now if you have the love and passion, and truly grasp that you are in the hospitality business, the third and last step you need to take (this is the longest, because it never ends)...learn, learn, learn. You get the most out of your job when you put yourself in a place of learning. I have had some success, but there is never a moment when I don't know that there is more for me to learn. I am constantly honing my craft, whether it is attending Bar Smarts seminars, distillery sessions, working on my Master of Mixology certification, or just sitting in another bar watching the staff, studying the back bar, and experiencing the moment.

If you pay attention to the three things I have outlined, then you are well on your way. Does this mean that you will be on the cover of *Wine and Spirits*? No, but it does mean that you will be a better bartender.

Oron Lerner, Mapal Bar, Haifa, Israel.

How presumptuous of me to think I can add anything to your own thoughts? I feel somewhat rude doing so, and still since you are a bartending role model I'll send my thoughts on the matter and hope you don't think I'm being arrogant.

The tough part is that situations and characters change, and at any one time a great bartender may need a completely different set of traits or habits to provide his guests with just the best kind of experience. So, the two things I can think of that are constant in great bartending characters of today are, first of all, love people.

Not anyone in particular, but people in general. This isn't exactly 'social' or 'friendly', these are people who enjoy company, an interesting chat or watching others and it cannot be fake, everyone feels it when it is. The best bartenders I know are like that, approachable, always there even after starring in a movie, judging cocktail competitions and writing two books simultaneously, they'll still find the time to make you a drink and make you feel important, because that's what we do behind the bar.

And the second thing is to love the drink. This isn't being an alcoholic, we're not drinking to forget, we're drinking truly because we enjoy the drink. It is preferable that you learn to love and appreciate all manner of drink, because when you enjoy that, you believe in what you're selling which then stops being a 'sale' and turns into entertaining your guests with nothing but the best and most fit a drink you can. Guests always drink more of what the bartender enjoys most.

I find it comforting that this job requires you to love. Both for people and the drink, what a happy vocation this is.

Tim Judge, Diageo Reserve Brand Ambassador, Africa (yes, the whole of Africa!).

I'm sure that I echo the comments of many seasoned bartenders around the world in saying that the keys to success are passion, dedication, a love of people and above all humility. Whilst the ability to stir two drinks at once whilst performing a Japanese hard shaken blazer is fantastic, the true measure of a bartender is in the relationships they build with each and every guest that walks through the door. It's not about how much you know, it's about how you make people feel.

Chapter 3

Barbacks: The Unsung Heroes of the Craft

We never had barbacks in the bars where I worked in the 1970s and 80s, though when I was at the North Star Pub in Manhattan's South Street Seaport we had porters who helped out behind the bar. They also did myriad other jobs in the kitchen, in the storeroom, and in the huge walk-in where we stored kegs of beer. (The walk-in belonged to a fishmonger at the Fulton Street Market around the corner, and we just rented a two-keg-wide area of it since the Pub's storage space was pretty minuscule.) I was a manager at the North Star, though I did jump behind the bar from time to time, and those porters were very imperative to giving decent service to the punters.

I've also worked with barbacks when I've pulled guest bartender shifts in recent years, and I've heard more than a few stories about how highly valued some of these guys are. This year I've decided to feature a few of them, as described by the bartenders they work with. If you have a favorite barback that you'd like to see highlighted in an upcoming project or publication, drop me a line at gaz@gazregan.com.

David Hickling
nominated by **Felix Crosse**, Head Bartender, **Alchemist**, Manchester, UK.

I run the bar of a busy cocktail bar restaurant in Manchester, UK. 25 percent of our sales are cocktails and they are molecular lead. The menu is not easy and the bar is designed to handle much less trade. The only reason we succeed at what we do is the support we have around us.

David Hickling is the best barback I have ever worked with. He was employed through head office family connections about 8 months ago. He came from no experience and spent the first two months squeezing limes and lemons in an uninspiring way. He learnt in a very inspiring way (His current nickname involves the word citrus for his epic squeezing) and became one of the most challenging and hopeful people I have ever worked with. He is currently 18 and has spent his accomplished time carrying more glasses and filling more juices than I could ever hope to. He is willing, without attitude and constantly full of it. Regardless, in the time I have known him has never been offended or put down by any comment I have to make. His attitude means no remark I make goes unreplied but always without malice or underhandedness. He and people like him are the reason why I go to work and I hope to have him be the one who replaces me.

He regularly makes me angry but not once have I had him say no without first making me ask why I ask him to say yes. I trust him implicitly regardless of alcoholic deviations and he is the first on my top ten staff to thank.

I see him growing and evolving before me and I'm reminded of where I came from, the times when I never thought I could make a daiquiri. I was holding a hosepipe in an alleyway when I first thought I could be a bartender and I see so much of this in him that I know regardless of his choices I will respect him regardless.

Ian Krupp
nominated by **Laura Lindsay**, **Providence**, Los Angeles, CA.

Ian is my favorite barback because he's MY barback. See, for the longest time I didn't have a barback. Then one magical day, management decided I shouldn't have to juice alone. Ian has quickly picked up how to juice, re-stock, and make simple drinks and is learning how to stir, shake, and make all the potions we serve at the bar. What's more important is that he has learned how to listen and ask the right questions to ensure the customer gets a drink they'll like and be happy.

Ian is my comrade-in-arms when we're knee-deep in service tickets with people eating nine-course dinners at the bar. See, my bar is inside a Michelin two-star restaurant, so our duties are bit intense at times: serving drinks, service orders, wine pairings, clearing and marking silver, and making people laugh is all in our night's work. I'm supremely happy to have a hard-working guy on my team and thought I'd take a moment to show an under-appreciated lot some appreciation.

Carlos Lopez-Flores
nominated by **Daniel Eun** and **Eric Alperin**,
The Varnish, Los Angeles, CA.

Daniel [pronounced DAN-yul] sez: Carlos is the greatest barback ever. It's not uncommon for guests at the Varnish to be at our bar and be struck by how fast, efficient, and graceful Carlos moves behind the bar. I've overheard something along the lines of, "the bartenders are cool, but look at that guy (Carlos) move!", more times than I can count. Considering the talent that we have had tending the bar at the Varnish, it's quite the testimony indeed when guests are more in awe of our champion barback than our bartenders.

Too many times when I work behind the stick (usually on weekends when we are as high-volume as the Varnish can possibly get) I find that my needs are being met as soon as I'm made aware of them: I'll be pouring the last bits of a bottle, when I look over and see Carlos already uncapping its replacement; I look over at our juices and before I can ask for more lime, Carlos is already pouring some more into my flask; I'm combining the ingredients for a hot drink into a glass when Carlos grabs it and takes it to the espresso machine to finish it off himself. Not only has he brought his own expertise, he has trained his brothers to follow his example as well. There's a reason why we all call him the true "boss" of the bar and why we all call him "Papa" with the respect that the term holds. Carlos is just...awesome.

Eric sez: I have always found the hospitality business to relate to dancing. It is a stage. Live theatre every night. And we are the players. Our motions of flair, elegance, and economy of movement dictate the evening. I have worked with many teams in my time, but it is my experience with Carlos that has solidified that the barback is more in charge of the inner workings of the bar than the surgeon (aka Bartender). Carlos is quick and agile. In his youth he was a champion mountain-hiker. He has told me of these competitions when he was younger and living in Mexico. Carlos's movements are deft and precise and the moment I turn a bottle over and expend its last drop there is another one to my right, cap removed and ready to rock. Locked and loaded I feel confident in the trenches with Carlos. He also brings his son in one shift per week to show him what his father does to prepare and open the bar. It warms my heart because of the legacy we share with each other at the bar he believes in it and is passing it onto his blood.

Raul Dominguez
nominated by **Meaghan Dorman**, **Raines Law Room**, New York City.

I work with a gem of a barback at Raines Law Room. Raul Dominguez has been with me for 3 1/2 years and is truly my right arm. Aside from the essential things like showing up on time, covering shifts, and being quick and efficient, Raul adds so much to Raines Law Room. He keeps me organized, always remembering to tell me when we are low on bottles and fruit. When we change the menu he helps me redo the ordering and bar setup to deal with the changes. Raul is studying to be a medical examiner, so the ugly parts of the job don't faze him at all. He just says cleaning a toilet or a backed up sink isn't even close to what he'll be seeing on the job, smiles and keeps moving. My proudest moment of Raul was on his 21st birthday when we asked him what he wanted to drink. He wanted a Manhattan and he made it himself, with no instructions. He'd watched us so many times he made a lovely Manhattan for himself.

Rudi Carraro,
nominated by Alex Kratena, Head Bartender, Artesian Bar at The Langham, London, UK.

Rudi Carraro, aka super carraro.com, is our executive barback. Rudi joined our team less than year ago, but I must admit he's the most amazing barback I've come across over my career. Not only he is flexible whenever we need him, but first of all he is faster than Speedy Gonzales.

His pro-active approach and passion make him learn fast, he is great at multitasking and already knows all our recipes (without being trained on them), he is well-dressed and -spoken, the only bad side of him is that he is more popular with ladies then the rest of bartenders at Artesian all together, which makes us upset. ☺

His organizational skills are unbelievable (the bloody bastard re-organized the entire spirit cellar since he started—he simply came with better system than mine.). His biggest asset, apart from executing his work duties, is that he is super funny and can easily imitate other colleagues and all the Langham management staff.

I'd be grateful if he makes it to top barbacks, because he definitely deserves it! (And probably next year will be working as bartender anyway...)

Pedro Ramirez
nominated by **Natalie Bovis**, The Liquid Muse, **Milagro**, Santa Fe, NM.

Our Barback, Our Hero, Pedro
by Natalie Bovis, The Liquid Muse

"I look calm. But, inside, sometimes I'm not." Pedro Ramirez is describing what it's like to be a barback. Our restaurant turns into a nightclub by 11 pm, accommodating an average of 300 people. We switch from crafted cocktails to turn-and-burn, and handle the crowd with 3 bartenders and 2 barbacks, selling hundreds of drinks. Barbacks set mise-en-place, stock beer, clear tables, keep ice bins filled, run to the upstairs liquor room repeatedly. Their reward when the club closes is to wash glasses, mats, sweep and mop floors. We close at 2, but by the time every bottle is wiped down, the money is counted, it's after 3:30 am. Pedro recalls, "The first night I cleaned until 5:15 am. I knew I had to become more organized."

Many bartenders start behind the scenes. My entrée to the world of hospitality was as a busser during high school vacations. I worked so unobtrusively that it didn't even require acknowledgement. But I knew that once I turned 21, I could be a bartender. I would have the power.

Pedro doesn't live with that same certainty. He grew up in a village in Guatemala. His first language is not Spanish, but a Mayan dialect. After his mother abandoned him as a baby, he lived with his grandmother until she passed away when he was 7. He stayed a short time with his biological father and his new wife, but the woman didn't feed or care for Pedro, so he ran away and worked as a child-laborer picking rice until he was taken in by a family in the town. He took English lessons and saved money from his own jobs until he had enough to come to America.

Shortly after arriving in Arizona at age 19, he contracted tuberculosis and wound up with blood-filled lungs in a five-day coma. He took months to recuperate, and by the time the doctor gave Pedro the OK to work, his roofing job was long gone. He thought he'd have to go back to Guatemala but a friend offered him a one-way ride to Santa Fe, New Mexico with the promise of work. After selling his only possessions—a

CD player and a boom box—Pedro managed to start a new life … again.

Pedro recalls the day he arrived in Santa Fe: "The town was all white. I had never seen snow. It was so beautiful, I cried." Despite his slight stature (about 5'2") Pedro did a variety of physically demanding odd jobs, which is how he wound up at our bar.

He was hanging from the ceiling setting up lighting equipment for a DJ who, as it turns out, often didn't bother to pay Pedro at the end of the night, leaving him to walk home hungry and without money. One of our bartenders, Alex Velez, noticed his hard work and heard his tale. At first, the bar manager didn't want Pedro as a barback because he can't reach the highest bar shelves, and struggles with English. Alex, who is from Puerto Rico, convinced him to give Pedro a chance.

The key to Pedro's success at his job is that he's intuitively professional. "No one has to tell me to be on time, not to do drugs or drink. I am 100 percent in the moment. Now, I train new barbacks. Andrew (Andrew Roy, a bartender) said, 'Pedro, you are my hero.' I don't have parents to say they are proud of me, but I am proud of myself. I buy clothes for work, things that I never thought of wearing. Like a tie. I never thought I would wear a tie. So now I think of myself differently."

Pedro says that through work, he is getting back what he has lost: "We are a family. I'm not handsome or good at speaking with the people, but I earned my place with my work. The bartenders can make more drinks, and the bar makes more money. I value my job and am proud to be part of this team."

gaz sez: Milagro, sad to say, has closed since Natalie wrote this piece. I hope that Pedro landed on his feet.

Chapter 4

Bartenders' Most Embarrassing Moments

Don Miguel Ruiz, author of *The Four Agreements* among other fabulous spiritual books, reminds us that even when we do our very best, our best isn't always as good as it was yesterday, or last week, and it's important that we don't beat ourselves up about that. Hence we're including this topic in our Mindful Bartending section this year. Learning to laugh at ourselves and not to take ourselves too very seriously is, I believe, integral to becoming a mindful bartender.

We've all had embarrassing moments behind the bar, right? We've said the wrong thing at exactly the wrong time or to the wrong person. And we've all messed up by knocking over drinks, dropping shakers, or screwing up that fabulous juggling move that we thought we'd perfected. And I've had more than my fair share of these, believe you me!

The incident that stands out in my mind as being the most embarrassing moment I ever endured behind the bar dates back to around 1974 or '75. It was a jam-packed-and-jumpin'

Friday night at Drake's Drum, the Upper-East-Side-of-Manhattan joint where I worked when I first hit the Big Apple.

The bar was six-deep and I was strutting my stuff, working as fast as I could, and trying to keep track of who should be the next punter to get served. A guy in his early twenties, clean-cut and neatly dressed, had been waving a double sawbuck ($20 US) at me for a while and I figured that his turn had come. I looked him dead in the eye: "What can I get you, mate?" I asked.

The guy turned out to be so drunk that he couldn't even form the words to give me his order. "Sorry, sir, I can't serve you tonight," I told him, and I walked down the bar to serve the tall blonde who had, in my estimation, been waiting for long enough. So what if she'd only just walked into the bar?

In Manhattan, and most other major cities I guess, there are so many bars that most people who get cut off don't even try to argue their case. They simply move on to the next bar to see if they can bluff a drink out of some other bartender. And if you move away from someone as soon as you cut them off, they don't really have a chance to argue anyway, right? That wasn't the case with this guy, though.

After serving the blonde, I turned to look down at the service end of the bar, and the guy I'd just refused to serve was standing there, glaring at me. The was no point putting it off, so I strode down the bar, gave him a steel-blade look, and asked what I could do for him. "Why won't you serve me?" he asked. But he didn't say it quite like that. The guy spoke with a severe stutter. He was, as far as I could tell, as sober as a judge.

Ever want the Earth to open up and swallow you?

God was good to me that night. She sent me the exact right thing to say. After he finished his protest, I gave him an astonished look and said, "Oh, dear. I'm terribly sorry, sir. You look very much like a guy I had to throw out of here last week, but now I can see you're not him. Would you let me buy you a drink to try to make up for my mistake?"

I'm not fool enough to think that this guy believed what I told him, but by accepting my apology, along with a large Johnnie Walker Black on the rocks I should add, he and I both saved face. It was a close call, though.

Enough from me, how about you? If you'd like to tell me about your most embarrassing moment behind the stick, write to me at gaz@ardentspirits.com, and I'll see what I can do about including your story in an upcoming publication. Here's my selection for this year—and there are some doozies. Promise.

Chris Edwardes, Hidden, Ibiza

I started working behind the bar in an American-owned restaurant in 1975, when I was 17. I was under the impression at the time that I was a cocktail bartender, we had a list of twelve cocktails (one of which was the Grasshopper and that one has remained on the lists of every bar that I have since been involved in since). Between 5:30 and 7 each day we had a happy hour (I never quite understood that surely it should have been a happy hour and a half). This was extremely popular—there would be a large queue of people waiting at the door and they would run up the stairs to get to the bar first to place their orders. Then, for the next hour and a half, the bar would be five deep.

On one particular night I had an order for four Piña Coladas and I placed all the ingredients into the large American blender on the bar top, added ice, and then turned it on full. Yes, you have guessed it, I neglected to put the top onto the blender. Piña Coladas went everywhere. I was completely white, and my silhouette was on the mirror behind me. I think that pretty much everybody was wearing a bit of Piña Colada that night. It was one of those moments when you want to just disappear into a large hole in the ground. I never made that mistake again.

> *gaz sez: I have a blender story, too! Circa 1974, the bosses at Drake's Drum decided that we needed a blender. All of the bartenders hated that, so after a couple of days the closing bartender—we stayed open till 4 a.m. every night—simply threw it into the garbage. The bosses didn't notice for a couple of days so they couldn't be sure who had done it. "I haven't seen it for days," said the bartender they questioned.*

They dutifully bought another blender, and that one, too, got thrown away. I think they went through at least four blenders before they threatened to fire a bartender at random if another one disappeared.

Joseph Albanese, Director of Beverage Operations, **Foxwoods Resort and Casino**, Ledyard, CT.

I was six months into my bartending career and I was on top of the world. I was working one of the hottest night clubs in Miami and money was no object. I had memorized every drink known to man and all of my regular's favorites. One slow night an elderly gentleman came in and said, "I will give you a $100 if you can tell me what's in a Greyhound." I rattled it off to him and he actually gave me the $100. The people at my bar were telling him that he couldn't stump me if he tried and were cheering me on. Then suddenly he asked, "How is Amaretto made?" That was it. Instantly I realize, I spent so much time memorizing cocktails and have not spent one minute trying to know what was in the bottles prominently displayed behind me. I felt like an idiot. I promised myself that would never happen again and went on a mission to learn everything about every bottle on the bar or that could be on the bar.

> *gaz sez:* Wise words here, guys. There's a good lesson in Joseph's story. Never stop learning, and try to cover all aspects of your craft.

Michael Parker, Manager and Head Bartender, Clydz Sidebar, New Brunswick, NJ.

I've been the manager and head bartender of clydz sidebar for about four years. It's a sexy little Prohibition basement all brick inside craft cocktail bar. We do this monster happy hour from 4 to 7 where everything on our 140-drink cocktail list is half price, from beer to a ramos gin fizz. So the bar is completely packed, like six-deep, and were running around like chickens in vests and ties with our heads cut off. I lock eyes with this girl that I have never seen before in there but that I would like to see way more of. She walks up and says something to the tune of, "do you like have some like hot cider stuff?" Now in my mind I feel like:

1. I'm no longer attracted to this girl from her shit drink order
2. I'm pissed because its busy as shit and now I have to leave the bar to go to the walk-in and find cider to then go to the espresso machine to heat it up and then to come up with a cocktail on the spot because we usually don't have or work with cider (it's in the heart of a snowy winter).

So I run in the back and grab the cambro with the cider, pour some into a footed mug, heat it and put some brandy and a bunch of other stuff into it. I hand it to the girl over the bar and go to the micros to start her a tab. By the time I turn around I hear this putrid noise over the ambient hum and music that's in the bar. I look to see that this girl has spit her first sip of the drink on the floor and has begun to vomit in the middle of bar. I shortly come to find out that in my rushing around I grabbed the wrong cambro. I accidentally filled this mug with strained liquid duck fat that we use to cook with in our kitchen. Just so you know, they happen to be the same exact color. Someone had put the cambro in the bar juices section of the walk-in. So after a bunch of apologizing and buying of drinks it ended up being all good, however it did give me my most embarrassing bartender story.

Robbie Wilson, SnugBar, Corvallis, OR.

I was working a rather busy Friday night, I work at a very small basement speakeasy bar so I'm the only one. I had batched two cocktails in one larger Parisian shaker and was going to town on it when my hands slipped, and it opened up all over me and one of my regular customers at the bar. We both were soaked. For a second I was sweating bullets, but he laughed it off and I gave him a towel to wipe himself off and his bill was on me that night.

> *gaz sez:* I googled Robbie Wilson after I read this story, and I found a fabulous article about him in The Corvallis Advocate. Here's a short clipping from same: "Through his interpretive drink making, Robbie teaches people that going out for a drink can be as wonderful as seeing Cirque du Soleil. With Robbie, you don't just ask for a drink, you ask for him to make something specific and he will shock you with how on the spot it is." www.covallisadvocate.com. Not too shabby, huh!

Dan Warner, Global On Premise Specialist, **Absolut Vodka**.

In June this year I was doing some Ambassador work for Absolut in Thessaloniki, Greece. A sweet gig in a beautiful part of a country that I love. When it got to the drinks bit I moved to the bar but the air conditioning was out of action so it was like 1,000 degrees in there. I was already sweating like Jimmy Savile in a clown outfit at a children's birthday party but then, when I was shaking out some Cosmopolitans, my sweaty hands lost purchase and suddenly instead of shaking the drink I was wearing it. All down my crisp white shirt. Right in front of 50 keen Greek bartenders. It was so embarrassing. Pink was never my colour. . . .

Johann Toffa,
Responsable entre deux places, Grenoble, France.

I'm not living a very exciting bartending life in my banned-bartending culture country, but the most embarrassing moment I've experienced was quite horrible. Two girls came to the bar and asked for a Mojito and a virgin ginger mojito. I prepared the drinks and went to the table, giving the drinks to each lady without event thinking about it. Soon came the remark: "I'm just fat, she is the pregnant one!"

Drinks are on the house, miladies . . .

Chris Halleron, **Duffy's Bar**, Hoboken, NJ.

One [embarrassing moment] that resonates was the time I got all terrier and was barking at a guy to stop standing on the barstool. He kept looking back at me like I was a f*^king idiot, so I came around the bar to sort him out and it turns out he was 7+ feet tall.

Of course there was also the time I had to physically remove a drunken, belligerent transsexual from the bar... but I'll save the tale of that epic battle for my own book!!! (Certainly not my proudest moment, but s/he was grabbing our male patrons by the bits—it had to be done. SPOILER: Trannies are like Medusa—once their wig comes off, they lose all their power.)

gaz sez: Great stories, Chris, and the second one reminds me of an incident I had back in 1974 when a transvestite hooker came into Drake's Drum, the joint I worked in NYC back then. He was huge—probably at least 6'4" and very muscular. He minced up to the bar and asked me where the ladies' room was, and I pointed down the bar telling him, "Second door on the right."

He headed toward the bathroom and one of my regulars said, "Gary! That was a man!" "You go tell him he's a man," I told him. . . .

Spyros Patsialos, **Faltso Bar**, Athens, Greece.

It was a full crowded evening, since we had a masquerade party. A young couple was arrived in the bar. Although I had a lot of orders, I said "hello" smiling to them, I served them two glasses of water and I asked them what they would like to drink. They told me that they had heard a lot about me and this is why the woman wanted to drink any cocktail that I would suggest. The man ordered a Jack Daniels on the rocks.

I was very happy to hear this compliment from a new client and I tried to do my best in order to satisfy her taste buds. After having my cocktail ready, I grabbed a bottle of Jack with a very fast move, and then I tried to make one of my favorite tricks with the bottle, you know flair kind of things. Unfortunately the bottle slipped away crashing with the cocktail that I had made for the woman. A few seconds later I saw the woman having her hands on her face and I thought that something REALLY BAD had just happened (I imagined a piece of glass in her eye). She left quickly to go to the WC. The man followed her. Two minutes later, they turned back. They smiled at me. Luckily, everything was fine.

Five years later I still remember that these two minutes were the most embarrassing moments of my life behind the bar....

> *gaz sez:* Spyros and I go back a few years now— we met at the G'Vine Gin Bartender competition in Cognac. He's also quite the filmmaker, too, and you can catch his stuff on www.huntingspirits.tv.

Dylan Yelenich, CSS, Big Orange, Little Rock, AR.

I had a couple at the bar and they were really into drinks and we had been talking serious cocktails for a while. I had asked them if they had ever had a "real sour" with an egg and they had not. At the time, I had a variation of a Singapore Sling on our menu but was using sloe gin as the main liquor (very red). The drink also had an egg white in it. I built the drink in my shaker and started dry-shaking the egg to emulsify and during the dry shake I had turned to look at the other end of the bar and put my back to our guests in question. Somehow the shaker during mid-shake came apart and the red, eggy liquid went all over the guests that were so excited to have this drink with an egg in it. I'm talking drenched white sweater and the meal soaked in egg, sloe gin and pineapple juice. I stood there, horrified. Then, they just started laughing hysterically. I started to clean up everything in a very meek manner and they just said, "Oh, don't worry about it. There's nothing you can do but laugh at this situation." They nonchalantly took up bar towels and began cleaning themselves and their area so I ran to the back and had the kitchen fly out new food and came back with food and more towels and they were already clean-ish and smiling. As I set the food down the gentleman says, "OK, I'm ready to finally try this drink, but this time I'd like it in a glass." I know this story sounds ridiculous, but it is 100 percent true.

> *gaz sez:* *The fact that this involved grenadine and eggs adds so much to this story!*

Raul Faria, Serendipity 3 at Caesar's Palace, Las Vegas, NV.

I was pretty busy at the bar one day and I was in the middle of a conversation with a guest when I noticed in my periphery two ladies grabbing stools at the end of the crowded bar. I went over and greeted them with drink menus and said, "How are we today, ladies? Would you like to see the food menu as well or are we just drinking?" and the one lady with her head down looked up and it was a guy that just happened to have a lovely long flowing mane, LOL. Oopsie!

> *gaz sez:* Don't laugh! It's happened to me. At airports, in theaters, and in shopping malls: "Excuse me, ma'am. Oops, sorry."

Chapter 5

Ladies Who Lush

by Francine Cohen

The Boy Scouts, Girl Scouts, summer camp, fraternities and sororities—all great places to make life-long friends with people who share similar interests, including giving back to the community. Only thing is, for most people, once you're past college age and getting deeper into your career, these kinds of opportunities to meet likeminded folks and make a difference together are few and far between.

Enter LUPEC. LUPEC (Ladies United for the Preservation of Endangered Cocktails) was started in Pittsburgh in 2000 by two friends who wanted to preserve that sense of camaraderie, share their interests in women's history and support the local community, all while having a great drink.

Only problem was, in Pittsburgh in those days (yes, not so long ago, but hey, remember that this post-Prohibition cocktail revolution is still in its early stages) the only place to find a decently made Old-Fashioned and its ilk was at "dirty old man bars." Founder, **Whiskey Daisy** (indeed, the LUPEC ladies have cocktail-derived code names), explains the genesis of the organization that grew from one chapter in the southwestern Pennsylvania, which started as a joke amongst friends, to multiple chapters with member rolls filled with female bartenders and spirits industry professionals around the country in cities like Boston, Denver, Houston, LA, NY, Philadelphia, San Francisco, and Chicago (which boasts two – a suburban and a city chapter). She says, "We started LUPEC basically because we all liked to drink. The whole idea was for us to hang out and talk about women's history and drink classic cocktails. Classic cocktails at the time weren't widely available. A lot of it was the 'get the sorority girl drunk' cocktail variety, but we had all moved past that or had never been there and didn't want a fruity drink that got you drunk. Options were limited. You could always get a G&T and the super basics, but 12 years ago, where were you going to find a Manhattan? Much less one that was well made, mind you. At the time you went to an old man bar and you got what you got. So we had this idea that you'd make great cocktails at home and have a meeting in your living room."

The location of these first meetings dictated the size of the LUPEC chapter. And while many chapters, like NYC's, have extended their roster beyond the Pittsburgh proscribed formula of "more than five or six, no more than 12" because as Whiskey Daisy notes, "How many can you fit in your living room?" the mission of the group is the same: enjoy great cocktails while learning something new, and hopefully professionally beneficial, along the way.

Of course, given the fact that many LUPEC women around the country are in the hospitality business and thrive on taking care of others at their bars and restaurants, the organization hums with charitable giving activities for various causes; LU-

PEC is a service organization that's about way much more than simply serving good drinks.

Hollis Bulleit of the Los Angeles chapter ascribes a certain amount of flexibility as a key to the success of this growing organization. She says, "LUPEC has worked because every region has defined itself based on its specific needs and social construct surrounding it."

Overall, LUPEC has become an outlet for women in the spirits and hospitality industry to get their social and professional needs met. From seminars on the history of women tavern operators (often the best way to raise a family and keep food on the table, believe it or not) to spirit tastings and education, LUPEC programming runs the gamut. **Lynn House** of the Chicago city chapter comments, "It has been an empowering forum allowing women to come together, share ideas and decompress for the stressful world we live in." Houston chapter founder **Alba Huerta** concurs, "LUPEC brings like-minded women together. We are all trying to achieve the same goals at different fronts. I see a lot of women coming into their own and making the decision to establish themselves as icons in their community."

Melanie and **Lizzie Asher,** founders of Pisco brand Macchu Pisco and LUPEC supporters and members themselves, recognize the value that LUPEC brings to its members. Melanie notes, "LUPEC has given me a forum to share best practices with other women producers and bartenders looking to start their own brands on a national level. It would be awesome and inspiring to see more women coalescing together behind and in front of the bar supporting each other."

Lizzie echoes her sister's sentiment and gets to the heart of how LUPEC can be a vehicle to success as she says, "We are women producers and brand owners. We are currently a very tiny minority of what is a multi-billion dollar industry. If we do not have women invading every facet of this spirits world, beginning with those behind the bar all the way into the boardroom, how can we possibly say we have equality in this world? Women supporting women is a key component of making that happen. What I find most interesting about LUPEC, that just as Macchu Pisco is doing, we are all opening paths in areas where women are as not as well represented in our industry i.e., behind-the-bar and at the top of corporate mastheads."

For LUPEC members around the country, this business and professional growth is invaluable. **Charlotte Voisey** of William Grant & Sons is one LUPEC supporter who has risen to great heights and sees her exposure as both positive and possible for others. She notes, "Every year, you're able to cite more and more examples of great women in the industry. Look at bartenders, or any career, actually, and there are more women, more good women, and more at the top of their game. It says women are just as capable as men to do well and rise to the top." Voisey continues, "Six years ago I could have named just three women leading the way, but now look at Speed Rack; we just did ten cities with sixteen top women competing in each."

That's progress. Progress for LUPEC and progress for the industry. Though sometimes, admittedly, it does get a little touchy. **Lynnette Marrero**, president of the New York City chapter, reveals, "There is a balance to be found as we go public with our programming because we do have to consider how we best promote women without obnoxiously pushing an agenda. The last thing we want to hear is 'Oh jeez, we're hearing about the girls again.'" House adds, "There has been some mocking from our male counterparts, they have even threatened to form their own group...Dudepec. I think it is hard for them to understand that women really need a place of their own some time."

If everyone acknowledges the need for "me" time that LUPEC provides, the agenda becomes less about the girls and more about the community. And then everybody wins.

Especially the charities that are the fortunate beneficiaries of LUPEC's charitable endeavors. Last year alone LUPEC members and supporters raised at least $100,000 for various local charities. **Kitty Amman**, a co-founder of the Boston chapter, confirms, "I doubt any of us will ever be in a position to, say, donate a wing to a hospital or a museum, but giving back to women in our community is something we all feel pretty passionate about. We're doing it the best way we know how!"

In Boston and in other cities, that help goes beyond simply planning fundraisers for events like Bottomless Closet, Dress for Success, MA Coalition Against Sexual Assault and Domestic Violence. More and more frequently, LUPEC ladies are called upon to create signature cocktails and host the bar at various events, and so often payment for the evening's work often comes in the form of a check made out to a charity near and dear to LUPEC's heart, while the LUPEC ladies donate their time and effort.

Joy Richard, a founding member of Boston's chapter, sees the far-reaching impact this combined effort of education, fundraising and mentorship has on the industry and their guests. She says about LUPEC's existence, "There's so much enthusiasm for raising awareness (in cocktail history and historic female figures), raising money (for local and national women's charities), and helping women rise up in the industry (bringing attention to female bartenders), and it's really catching on! It's amazing how many fantastic female bartenders I alone have met through the organization, let along how many amazing women have been brought into the limelight for nonindustry folks to see, because of this. Locally, I have seen such an amazing amount of enthusiasm for what we do as industry professionals and as philanthropists, and it just continues to grow."

Amman proudly concludes, "We're becoming a force to be reckoned with. There have always been women in this industry, as we learned while researching our *Ladies Behind Bars* seminar about the history of female bartenders. They just haven't always been treated with the same respect, courtesy, or level of professionalism as men. But hey, there's plenty of industries where that is the case. What we're seeing now are more female mixologists moving into leadership roles, opening and running amazing bars, and training future generations. And that's only going to continue. It's the mentorship that is really going to blow things up for women in this business, though, I think. And I hope that LUPEC can play a part in that, cultivating community and a space where you can learn about cocktails and commiserate about your experiences in the industry."

So, while our scouting badges and bunk field trip days may be behind us, the future is bright for the industry with LUPEC ladies in the mix.

> *gaz sez: When I started working behind the bar in New York, in 1973, I knew only one woman bartender. Her name was Rusty, she was good at what she did, accepted by all of us male bartenders, and she ran a tight ship (I can't remember the name of the joint she worked but it was an Upper-East-Side neighborhood joint).*
>
> *Bar owners, though, even those who knew and liked Rusty, very rarely considered hiring women to work the stick. Their excuses were that women couldn't lift heavy buckets full of ice, couldn't deal with unruly customers, break up fights, etc. I won't even go into how wrong they obviously were—that's a given.*

For the Ladies of LUPEC to pull off what they've pulled off, though, is just fabulous, and as Charlotte Voisey pointed out in Francine's article, the number of prominent women in our industry just keeps growing and growing. I LOVE the twenty-first century!

Thanks, Francine, for writing this piece, documenting a little bit of history, and for contributing it, free of charge, to this book. This boy loves you. Don't you forget it.

Chapter 6

Nothing Like a Dame

> "Money and ego massage are what motivate most beginning male bartenders, but that a job they are passionate about is what motivates most women in most jobs, full stop. Many a male bartender would countenance a drop in income if he could maintain his level of social status; most women, sensibly, don't give as much of a shit about that. Me saying A does not disprove the existence of B, of course: there are undoubtedly a lot of ego-driven female bartenders out there, and many male bartenders who care nothing for being the toast of the town." —Philip Duff, 4Bars.com.au, 2013.

Yes, I deliberately chose a title for this chapter that might just rattle a few cages, or at least grab a little attention, but I believe that I'm one of the least sexist people I know. And I freely admit that that hasn't always been the case, but even back when my generation, boys and girls alike, believed on the whole that women cooked and men dug ditches, I never bought into that wholeheartedly. When the women's liberation movement of the sixties was in full swing, I sided one-hundred-percent with the dames. Er, women . . .

When I first started tending bar in the 1970s, there were few women bartenders on the Upper East Side of Manhattan, but things have changed considerably since then. Here in the second decade of the twenty-first century, more than a few of the very best bartenders in the world are women, and as Mr. Duff says, a goodly number of them are behind the stick because they have a true passion for the craft.

Indeed, whereas lots of guys might go work behind a bar in the hopes of getting laid, most of the women back there fight a constant battle against their male customers who are constantly coming onto them.

So, aside from fending off usually-unwelcome advances, what are the other challenges facing women bartenders these days? There's only one way to find out. Ask 'em. And ask 'em I did. Here's what a bunch of them had to say.

Aisha Sharpe, Mother's Ruin, New York City.

How long have you worked behind the bar?

17 years.

Which bars, and where are they?

All in NYC: 277, BEDNY, Theo, Crobar, The Vi, Soho House, Good World (I'm probably forgetting a few . . .).

Has being a woman helped or hindered you as your career has progressed?

Not that I have anything to compare it to, but I would say help. I am a bit of a wise ass and I have always felt like I have been able to get away with a lot more of my wise ass remarks as a woman.

The nineties were an odd time as a woman bartender. Managers would go from having no women behind their bars to hiring a lot of talentless women who looked the part. When they discovered that these women couldn't bartend, they would stop hiring women altogether instead of hiring women who could actually do the job. I went on many interviews where they told me they weren't hiring any women. I got around this a couple times by suggesting they have me trail one night to prove myself, at no cost to them. That often worked.

Women on average have more taste buds than men, so that alone is an advantage.

What do you love, and what do you hate, about the way in which customers treat you, as a woman, when you are behind the bar?

Again, I have nothing to compare it to. I have never been a man behind the bar or anywhere else for that matter.

What advice would you give to other women who want to become bartenders?

Do it, it's one of the greatest jobs in the world. And never let anyone tell you you can't or you are not good enough. This advice is for men and women.

What do you think has been your greatest contribution to the craft?

My Negroni, of course.

Any particularly embarrassing moments stand out?

This happened within the first couple months of my first bartending job, which is perhaps why it was so embarrassing. I think the more seasoned one gets, the better one handles even the most humiliating situations. So what happened was...

The owner of the restaurant I was working at had a friend at the bar and they both ordered bottled beer. I decided to pull a move I thought would make me look really cool, a move I probably learned watching Cheers. I slid the beers down the bar to them, but given the rough surface of the bar, the bottles never made it to them, but the beer did. They both ended up soaked and I ended up humiliated, but I somehow managed to keep my job.

How do you prepare for a shift?

I always walk to work. It gets me in the right head space. Then I take my time setting up. I make sure to get to work a little early so I don't need to rush. I hate to start a shift in a frantic state, it takes so long to get your groove after that. I used to change my clothes as soon as I got to work, that used to be my way of getting my head in the game, almost like an athlete putting on a uniform. But now, I start the preparations on my way to work.

What's the most important aspect of tending bar for you?

I love the interaction with people I otherwise may not have the opportunity speak with. I love hosting people and help them have a wonderful evening. I love introducing them to new flavors. I like making people happy.

Anta Lubarte Rosen, LOLA, Great Neck, NY.

How long have you worked behind the bar?

Since 1999 in NY, 5 years prior in Riga, Latvia and Celebrity Cruise Line US (1997-99).

Which bars, and where are they?

Blaggard's Pub, NYC; Bistro Lamazou, NYC; Smorgasbord, NYC; Bistro Persil and Sage, Bellmore, NY, and LOLA, in Great Neck, NY (3+years).

Has being a woman helped or hindered you as your career has progressed?

Hmm…it is different in every place, for the most part helped, except for Lamazou, where they decided they wanted younger person behind the bar—and now the place is closed. [This] might not answer the question but I just wanted to share this situation.

What do you love, and what do you hate, about the way in which customers treat you, as a woman, when you are behind the bar?

Probably working behind the bar [at a] pub was less pleasant than in a lovely restaurant bar although that made my experience stronger and I learned to disregard some unpleasant situations and act accordingly. One thing I learned to be careful about: guy-customers tend to think if I am friendly and polite to them they can ask me out on a date and when politely I say no, I might lose a customer. What's up with that?

What advice would you give to other women who want to become bartenders?

Be confident, have a good manners, always have your hands/nails well-polished or just clean (many times I noticed this problem in female servers/bartenders), and learn, learn, learn every time you have a chance.

What do you think has been your greatest contribution to the craft?

I am proud to be part of this community, I am honestly enjoying taking care of the bar, my customers are my guests, I am dedicated to introduce my clientele to new or less known spirits, wine and more. I work behind the bar not far from NYC, in Great Neck, and we try to be a less traditional bar than most of the bars on Long Island. We prove that you don't have to travel far to have a great cocktail!

How do you prepare for a shift?

First of all, I do try to arrive to work happy, no matter what problems I might have I leave them out. I check all my spirits, syrups, juices, wines and beers to make sure I have them all stocked up. I make sure the bar is clean, not only the surface, also behind the bar, I set my tools and now I wait for my guests.

Any particularly embarrassing moments stand out?

Well, most recently on very busy Saturday night I had more than 7 drinks in my mind to make, [as well as] a few dinner orders to type into the computer, and as I am listening to a party of four calling their drinks I turn around and suddenly I only remember two of them. [It was a] terrible feeling to go back to them and apologize, but at the end it was all good. As I always say, people are understanding for the most part.

What's the most important aspect of tending bar for you?

Quality in both service and product; paying attention to details, and not forgetting to have a good time.

Cara Passarelli, Max Burger, West Hartford, CT.

How long have you worked behind the bar?

11 years.

Which bars, and where are they?

Loco Perro, East Hampton, CT; Baci Grill, Cromwell, CT; On the Border, Rocky Hill, CT; Max Fish, Glastonbury, CT; Max Burger, West Hartford, CT.

Has being a woman helped or hindered you as your career has progressed?

Both. Some may argue that sex appeal plays a part, but, though it may be an asset, I never learned to depend on it. There was a time at Fish when I was the only female on a team of 6 bartenders. I rose to the occasion and built quite a loyal following of guests of all types, ages, and sexes.

I have found it difficult to be taken seriously as a female bartender at some places I worked, and found it celebrated at others. I have encountered personality clashes with men at work that I would say could quite possibly have been due to sexism. But I believe it has always had more to do with the men feeling threatened and more concerned with protecting themselves and other men within the company. So, yes I have encountered sexism and adversity, but I have never allowed this to define or hinder me.

What do you love, and what do you hate, about the way in which customers treat you, as a woman, when you are behind the bar?

I do love being complimented, as all women do, on my hair, smile, whatever. However, most of all I just love being complimented on my drinks. This is the best. This is when it doesn't matter if you're a man or a woman, just that you got it right! I don't love all the compliments I get when behind the bar. It always gets uncomfortable when you have to grin and bear it through a line-crossing barrage of flirtation from an unwanted goggly-eyed guest. I find sexism so odd, if a person does a great job, treats you the way you want to be treated, then why on earth does it matter if they are a man or woman. As shocking as it may be, this sexism does exist. However all of this mild aggravation just gets filed under "general pains in the ass" for me.

What advice would you give to other women who want to become bartenders?

"Illegitimis non carborundum"—Don't let the bastards get you down! Stand up to adversity and know your value. If you love what you do, you are a very important asset to your bar, even if no one tells you so. Do not rely on others for validation, know you have the skill, personality, and tenacity to succeed. Never second-guess yourself, ever. The customer may always be right, but know that you may be as well! This applies more to your all-over interaction with others, in the industry and out of it. Own your female intuition; let it guide you. Make decisions for yourself that will support your beliefs and goals.

What do you think has been your greatest contribution to the craft?

I believe my inspiration and sense of knowing is what has separated me thus far. I delight in "getting it right," just knowing which cocktail in my arsenal will satisfy each guest. I work off of inspiration. When an idea comes to me it is fresh and new and if it really grabs a hold of me I know it will be a winner…for someone at least! More than this, however, it may be that I actually care that each guest is treated as an individual, someone special.

How do you prepare for a shift?

It all happens in the shower. Seriously. My head swims with ideas when I'm showering before work. What new ingredients do we have on bar? What was that great bar we visited last week? What was that great idea I read about this morning? What was that amazing flavor medley going on at dinner last night? I am usually dashing to my notebook before I've fully dried off! At work it's frantically putting all the parts together the way I see fit so that the result is a well-oiled machine ready for any happy-hour onslaught, late-night meltdown, and everything in between.

Any particularly embarrassing moments stand out?

The worst was the night I forgot to charge a couple of very well liked, respected, and regular bar guests for their second bottle of Opus One. Painfully going over with my manager how to approach the situation (I initially just paid for it out of pocket). In the end I told them at their next visit, ultimately collecting, and turning ten shades of red as they laughed it off. Thank goodness for those great guests!

What's the most important aspect of tending bar for you?

Joy. Joy in a guest's face when I've fully satiated their palate. The joy of learning and discovery. The joy of succeeding after much trial and error. That special kind of joy that creeps in when you have emerged, just a head above the weeds and, although buried, you know you own the night, the bar, and the smiles on everyone's faces!

What am I missing? What would you like to add? What inspires you?

Inspiration is the name of my game, be it food, history, stories, the season, a name, a time, or just the vibe of a certain place. When something inspires me I instantly think: "How would this moment, this place, this event, taste in a glass?"

What do you see for the future of women in bartending?

I would like to see all bartenders, women and men, be taken more seriously. I would also like to see a more level playing field, more acceptance for serious female bartenders. Women bring balance to an all-male bar, and one that can hang with the boys should be respected. One that can lead the boys—genius!

What is your favorite cocktail right now?

A solid Hendrick's Gin Negroni w/ Campari, Carpano, and a big ol' orange twist. One that's been barrel-aged at Max Fish—heaven.

Cari Hah, Coles Red Car Bar, Los Angeles, CA, and Neat Bar, Glendale, CA

How long have you worked behind the bar?

Collective 5 years.

Which bars, and where are they?

Dragonfly, Chicago; Izakaya Fu-Ga, Los Angeles; Blue Whale, Los Angeles; Varnish, Los Angeles; Neat, Glendale, and Coles Red Car, Los Angeles.

Has being a woman helped or hindered you as your career has progressed?

Helped and hindered!

What do you love, and what do you hate, about the way in which customers treat you, as a woman, when you are behind the bar?

It depends on the type of bar. I hated working as a woman at the club (Dragonfly in Chicago) because male customers treated me like a piece of meat. Sometimes at the craft bars, customers don't think I can make proper drinks because I don't have a mustache or wear stays. I love that customers may sometimes be more willing to talk to me about their ignorance of drinks and spirits because I may seem more approachable than my male counterparts, and when I do gain their trust in making great drinks they will return again and again and always ask for me.

What advice would you give to other women who want to become bartenders?

Respect the bar, respect yourself. Don't give into the stereotypical "sleep your way to the top" behavior. Carry yourself with grace and dignity.

What do you think has been your greatest contribution to the craft?

I see talent and even if the bartender is "lesser known" I want everyone to know how awesome they are and spread the news and love of that person. Also I work DAMN hard and always am willing to put in more than anyone else. And I'm an agave fairy. I fight for agave rights and will always do so.

How do you prepare for a shift?

Mentally I prepare myself to serve any kind of customer. I almost try to empty myself of ME. Whatever kind of day I've had, if I'm tired, sleepy, hungry, sad, depressed, etc., I drain all those emotions so I don't let those things affect my interaction with my coworkers and my customers. It's not about me during the shift. Everything is about the customers and the drinks.

Any particularly embarrassing moments stand out?

A possum the size of a dog wandered into my bar and I had to chase it around the bar and out with a stupid little muddler because it was the first thing I grabbed! I must have looked like an idiot chasing this HUGE possum around the bar!

What's the most important aspect of tending bar for you?

Ensuring that I am pleasing everyone around me and making sure that people are having a great time and have a great experience when they are in attendance. I also believe in spirits and letting their true essence shine through the way the distillers intended. I don't believe in covering the flavor of spirits so that you "don't taste the alcohol" the flavor of the spirit should be an element of the overall flavor of the cocktail.

What am I missing? What would you like to add?

I think that women biologically have a more discerning palate…this helps us to develop and describe tastes that maybe men may not be able to. This helps in cocktail creation. We are also more sensitive and feeling creatures which helps us to read customers better. Women are awesome bartenders!!!

Carol Donovan, HEARTY, Chicago, IL

How long have you worked behind the bar?

15+ years.

Which bars, and where are they?

All in Chicago, IL: Twin Anchors, The "GA" (German American), P.O.E.T.S. (stood for "Piss on everything tomorrow's Saturday"), Torre del Greco, Underground Wonder Bar, Mondelli's on Oak, Tommy's Chicago Bar & Grill.

Has being a woman helped or hindered you as your career has progressed?

I haven't thought about it in that way, actually. It certainly helped get the job to be a well-built woman when I was younger—I wasn't expected to have a brain or to do anything but get men to part with their money. But, while I was doing that I was learning and developing my talent.

As I've gotten older, it has been a little harder to get the opportunities that used to be handed to me just due to my looks. It's certainly not limited just to this industry, but looks remain a large part of how one is judged and given opportunities. Also, the perception of age as a detriment seems to come into play for women at a much earlier age than for men.

On the other hand, because I am a woman I am aware that there are certain situations I can diffuse much more easily than a man can. I have a better chance of charming a patron out of the undesired action, where a man in the same situation might have to use confrontation rather than diffusion.

I never want to have the thought that there is anything I can't do because I am a woman, so I do not want to think in the terms this question addresses. At the same time, I want to have an awareness that there are many options to get where you're going and sometimes the best one will be to play the "female card" or use those talents which are innately feminine.

What do you love, and what do you hate, about the way in which customers treat you, as a woman, when you are behind the bar?

I enjoy welcoming people into the bar, so I'm not sure I notice that they treat me differently than they treat anyone else. I expect customers to be respectful, but playful fun is fine—therefore there may be a lot of verbal innuendo going on, but it's a look-but-don't-touch policy usually. For the most part, I believe you get what you expect out of people, so I try to keep my expectations positive. Because of that, I find that other patrons will back me up if there is ever a problem (and there rarely is).

I had a situation recently where two men came in together and were quite flirtatious and somewhat louder than we are used to anyone being at our establishment. I was handling it by making them feel as if they were getting something but making it their "last and you'll have to go," and everything would have been fine. Unfortunately, the acting manager on the restaurant floor felt the need to deal with them without asking me whether I required his help and turned the whole thing into a conflict, which never had to be. Not only that—he kicked them out and told them they didn't have to pay, so we had some unnecessary lost revenue. Sometimes women's approach to diffuse is much more effective than men's approach of confrontation.

What advice would you give to other women who want to become bartenders?

- Be sure that you enjoy people—they're what this is all about.
- Treat people at your bar as you would guests in your home and you'll be fine.
- Remember that you are always on display while behind the bar—anything you do can be seen by guests so at all times remain professional.
- Learn not only drink recipes, but spirit categories so that you can know what tools you have to work with.
- Be organized behind the bar—once you have your bearings begin to think about how you can do two things at once to become more efficient.
- For women, this business is not all about boobs, but be prepared for the men who objectify female bartenders—pity them, but do not get a chip on your shoulder

about it. Have respect for yourself and demand it of your guests, but not in a confrontational way.
- You'll need a sense of humor to lean on often with the unusual things that happen when you're behind a bar.
- Keep in mind that as a female bartender you are part mom, part cop, part psychologist (you listen better than anyone), part unattainable dream girl, part manager—all while making delicious cocktails and making the register ring.
- Some great advice I have heard is to be sure to read the paper every day, so that you can speak to any topic a guest wants to bring up.
- While you will become very good at reading people, do not pre-judge anyone who comes into your establishment. Welcome all equally cordially, provide the same service, and you never know who you might be speaking with.

Special note: Should you find yourself with a confrontation in the bar, I have found that women have a tool men never can: the Mommy voice. In the midst of a fist-fight, using the scolding Mommy voice can get through to a drunk person in a way that trying to pull the combatants apart cannot. "Stop that right now, boys" as if you're talking to children somehow gets through to a drunk brain and can pause the action long enough to diffuse the situation.

What do you think has been your greatest contribution to the craft?

I think that my contribution is mostly to the guests I encounter. In addition to hospitality I want to demystify cocktails for them. Most do not want to make them themselves, but they enjoy knowing that they could. I want people to know that what we do is not magic, just knowledge and skill partnered with a strong desire to make them happy.

I also want them to know that they don't have to like every cocktail nor drink one that they do not like. I tell/teach them their opinion is valid, and that I am there to make them something they'll really enjoy not just to put on a song and dance show for them. At the same time, I teach them how to communicate with their bartender so that they get something they'll enjoy everywhere they drink. Don't drink a drink you don't like, but here is how to send it back so that the bartender understands what they can do to make you happy. Or, here is how to ask about the cocktail list so that you can select one you'll enjoy.

How do you prepare for a shift?

In addition to all of the regular prep (garnish, stocking, cleaning, glassware, etc.), I try to spend some time feeling positive energy about everyone I am about to encounter. Communicate with the universe that I am here, ready to serve, and ready to enjoy whatever the night may bring.

I try to bring extra "emergency" items with me, which are not usually part of the tools at the bar (including, but not limited to: stain remover, tweezers, lighter/matches, antacid, ibuprofen, bobby pins, safety pins, spare button, band-aids, phone charger, breath mints, standard size batteries—anything that a guest might suddenly need but not have). If I can save the day I have provided a service above the expected which will cause a guest to remember and want to return. I get to be a hero in a small way and the guest has a memorable experience.

Any particularly embarrassing moments stand out?

I am not easily embarrassed, so this is a challenging for me. Probably some of my early days of bartending, when I was in the "fake it till you make it" position. I know there were times when I had to pull out the Mr Boston's and read the recipe—and just hope I was making what the guest wanted. There was no training when I started—you just jumped back there and made mistakes until you didn't any more.

During a time in the industry when Martinis had just become vodka rather than gin, I did not often get a call for Manhattans. I definitely made some very bad drinks for some very understanding customers who allowed me to "correct" the drink more than once before they could consume it!

What's the most important aspect of tending bar for you?

Put the guest first. Offer hospitality plus something they did not expect. It's not about me—it's about the person in front of me. My ego does not have any place behind the bar. I need to be an amazing hostess first and foremost.

I see so many bartenders putting on a show, and feeding on the energy of being on stage and the center of attention, but that is flawed and will not lead to long-term success.

I think the key to stellar service is to feed on the energy of making people happy! Your guests may not know why they enjoy your bar more than others—but they know they want to return because the experience was so amazing.

What am I missing? What would you like to add?

If you are a female behind the bar, some part of your job is to be a sex object, and if you're not okay with that this is not the profession for you! If you have a chip on your shoulder or need to campaign for equal rights, this is probably not the career for you. The most successful female bartenders get to be both expert drink-maker and object of admiration at the same time. When people want to see you and want to drink what you're making—then you know you've found that balance.

If you think you're going to spend time "educating" men about how to properly treat women, the bar is not the place from which to do that (except by example).

By the same token, if you respect yourself then you can command proper respect from guests while still having room to joke and have fun with them. It is on that fine indistinguishable line where the female bartender is most successful.

Cheryl Charming, aka Miss Charming, Bourbon O Bar in the Bourbon Orleans Hotel, New Orleans. LA.

gaz sez: This joint was open in time for Tales of the Cocktail, 2013, and it was the best bar I visited all week. Don't visit NOLA without popping in to see Miss Charming!

How long have you worked behind the bar?

Since 1980.

Which bars, and where are they?

Too many to mention, but I tended bar in Arkansas, Texas, Washington, Oregon, California, and Arizona, but the bulk of my bartending career was on a cruise ship in the Caribbean and at Walt Disney World.

Has being a woman helped or hindered you as your career has progressed?

I don't believe gender has helped or hindered. It's all about the person.

What do you love, and what do you hate, about the way in which customers treat you, as a woman, when you are behind the bar?

First, customers can treat me anyway they choose. I don't take their behavior personally, and I feel it has nothing to do with my gender. I've trained bartenders to have duck feathers. My job is to get customer/guests' money out of their pockets and into my register because the goal is sales and I do "whatever it takes" to meet that bottom line. Doing "whatever it takes" can be as simple as a smile, but it can also mean a little entertainment, remembering their name, eye contact, humor, but basically, providing the best customer experience I can for that customer/guest.

What advice would you give to other women who want to become bartenders?

Be able to do all the work required for the position. This includes carrying cases of beer, taking out the trash, etc. If you are working with a male bartender then closing duties can be shared. Females can clean and count the bank while males can tend to the trash and heavy duties. But, it should never be taken for granted. Females should always be able to do ALL duties of a bartender.

What do you think has been your greatest contribution to the craft?

Since 1998, I've provided basic tips and advice for up-and-coming bartenders via my website, www.misscharming.com. It's been a labor of love, and I'm honored to help.

How do you prepare for a shift?

The first ten years of bartending I never thought about it. But, soon I learned that being behind the bar was similar to being an actor on stage. To be on stage, in a fishbowl, or whatever you compare it to takes energy. So, I learned to carve out time to find a quiet space and mediate before my shift. I also take about 15 minutes to stretch. It's just a choice that works for me.

Any particularly embarrassing moments stand out?

I don't have an embarrassing moment. But if the question was craziest moment, funniest moment, or memorable moment then I'd have answers to share J.

What's the most important aspect of tending bar for you?

Customer service.

What am I missing? What would you like to add?

1. Know the bottom line. (In case you don't know, the bottom line is sales.) More sales is a win-win for the owner and you.
2. Work like a swan. Swans appear elegant and in control on the surface, but are padding like hell under the water to make things happen.
3. Be a team player and never lose sight of the big picture.
4. Understand that there's not one person (in the whole world) that knows everything. Every bar I work, I learn something new.
5. See the good in everything. One example is while hauling out the trash. Thank the heavy dripping trash bag. It represents a good shift that put money in your pocket that provided income for your livelihood.

Cris Dehlavi, M Restaurant and Bar, Columbus OH.

How long have you worked behind the bar?

Total—20 years. At M, 10.

Which bars, and where are they?

M Restaurant and Bar, Columbus, OH; Mouton, Columbus, OH; Pie's Gourmet, Columbus, OH; and Metropolitan Grill, Tucson, AZ.

Has being a woman helped or hindered you as your career has progressed?

I would say mostly it has helped. I am in the right time to be a woman behind the bar as we now garner much respect.

What do you love, and what do you hate, about the way in which customers treat you, as a woman, when you are behind the bar?

I love being a woman behind the bar. I feel like people very much respect my craft and love for creating cocktails and I believe as long as you keep it classy a little flirty smile goes a long way. The only thing I can say I hate is the occasional sexist comment but I have learned how to professionally stop that immediately.

What advice would you give to other women who want to become bartenders?

I would tell them to learn as much as they can about bartending and crafting cocktails. There is no respect for the female bartender who only uses her looks as opposed to her skills.

What do you think has been your greatest contribution to the craft?

My greatest contribution has been the ability to not only craft a delicious cocktail but also that I have learned a lot about the history of cocktails and love sharing that with my guests at the bar.

How do you prepare for a shift?

I try to set myself up for total success before a shift, prepping, stocking, etc. I also plan to be completely ready 10 minutes before service so that I can get my mind in the right place ☺.

Any particularly embarrassing moments stand out?

I picked up a store/pour from the neck, it was full of simple syrup, and the lid was not attached. The entire bottom dropped out, simple syrup went EVERYWHERE, and I slipped and fell right on my ass in front of a full bar.

What's the most important aspect of tending bar for you?

Corny as it may sound, it is developing relationships with my guests, building regulars, and memorizing what they like, drink, and THEIR NAMES.

What am I missing? What would you like to add?

Only that I think it is critical to surround yourself with other people who love what you love—go to Tales, MCC, etc.....subscribe to blogs written by bartenders, get involved in USBG. I learn from people every day—from new bartenders to the big names in our industry.

Emily Chappelle, Bryant's Cocktail Lounge, Milwaukee, WI.

How long have you worked behind the bar?

I've been at Bryant's for four and a half years, have been bartending for seven years.

Which bars, and where are they?

All of the bars I have tended are in Milwaukee: Circle A, House of Frankenstein, Frank's Power Plant, Cactus Club, Victoria's, Odd Duck, and currently Bryant's Cocktail Lounge.

Has being a woman helped or hindered you as your career has progressed?

A little bit of both; most bars I've worked at require a pretty face and little-to-no skill when it comes to cocktails. My current position at Bryant's Cocktail Lounge requires speed, accuracy, and knowledge of hundreds of cocktails, so when a customer requests a man to make his drink (which has happened several times) I find it insulting because I happen to be the fastest bartender we have, with an encyclopedic knowledge of cocktails.

On a positive note, however, there was one situation where two men told me (after a few rounds) that when they walked in they were disappointed to see a woman behind the bar because they figured an attractive female was just that and nothing more, but they were amazed with their cocktails and apologized for judging me before I even started mixing. If I can change one man's mind about lady bartenders in general, then I think I'm doing just fine.

What do you love, and what do you hate, about the way in which customers treat you, as a woman, when you are behind the bar?

Like I said above, I love it when I can "wow" someone who previously doubted my skill. I hate, hate, HATE when people can't distinguish between polite chit-chat and flirting. I've had many work-stalkers over the years (both men and women) and it makes my job difficult to be uncomfortable behind the bar while still remaining chipper.

What advice would you give to other women who want to become bartenders?

Read cocktail books! Even if you work in a typical beer-and-a-shot joint, the more you know about liquor and mixing, the better. Always have a few standard classics under your belt. My biggest pet-peeve about bartenders is not knowing how to make a Manhattan, because it's three ingredients that every bar has.

What do you think has been your greatest contribution to the craft?

I absolutely love coming up with new cocktails, and I've contributed at least 30 original creations to the Bryant's menu. Speaking of which, Bryant's has no physical menu, so each drink order is a conversation about what the customer likes/dislikes, which makes it easier to come up with new drinks as opposed to wasting product.

How do you prepare for a shift?

I generally come in about an hour and a half before we open, clean the bathrooms, set out garnishes and fruit juices, juice lemons and limes, make whipped cream, blend coconut cream, cut fruit, make syrups, take out the recycling, wash any leftover dishes, put on my vest and turn on the open sign.

Any particularly embarrassing moments stand out?

I guess I don't get embarrassed that easily, so I'd have to say, on my first day ever bartending at a bar called Circle A, someone ordered a rum and coke and I asked my co-worker how to make it.

What's the most important aspect of tending bar for you?

I want everyone to be comfortable, so I try to be as fast as possible while still making sure that the cocktails are delicious.

Gabriella Mlynarczyk, INK, Los Angeles, CA.

How long have you worked behind the bar?

26 years on and off.

Which bars, and where are they?

Ink, Los Angeles; Eva, Los Angeles; Café Habana, NYC; Woodson & Ford, NYC; Table 50, NYC; Rocking Horse, NYC; French Roast, NYC; Limelight, NYC; Criterion, London, and Café De Paris, London.

Has being a woman helped or hindered you as your career has progressed?

Mixed, it's the same old story. As a woman bartender you are not taken as seriously as the boys, you don't fit into the boys club of management usually, and if you want to progress you need to work 20 times harder to get noticed for your skill rather than your looks.

I also dislike that an employer will not want to give you extra tasks because they think as a woman you won't be able to handle the workload, on the contrary we are pre-programmed to be multi-tasking goddesses and it should be the reverse. Recently, however I feel a shift, that women are being given their due especially behind the bar.

Male egos also tend to clash so two of my previous employers like to have someone that has less arrogance that some men unfortunately like to display when their back is against the wall, and they both hired me because they wanted someone that had more of a nurturing and sympathetic side to them as well as for my creative skills.

What do you love, and what do you hate, about the way in which customers treat you, as a woman, when you are behind the bar?

I dislike when I am not considered to have a valuable enough opinion on a spirit brand, wine or beer. Male customers tend to ask the boy behind the bar for their opinion first, usually the boy behind our bar will turn to me to ask my opinion and then the customer is surprised by the info I give them. As a woman too you are expected to be all bubbly and smiling, when the shits hit as they do on a busy night I am someone that tends to put my head down and focus on getting everyone served rather than spending time flirting, and as a woman sometimes that can be perceived as being cold.

I love that people are impressed by the fact that a woman bartender can be put in charge of a bar program that needs to complement a very modern menu, on the lighter side I love the flirtatious aspect of my job and employing that old adage "you get more bees with honey."

What advice would you give to other women who want to become bartenders?

With anyone I would recommend studying your spirits, get to know what you are selling, let your passion for the craft show, give it 100 percent of your effort or don't bother, as a woman get ready for a bumpy ride when it comes to dealing with some male bar managers especially if you want to progress, and use your smarts instead of your looks to get to where you need to go, ultimately you will get more respect for it.

What do you think has been your greatest contribution to the craft?

I use a few progressive culinary techniques to make most of my drinks, two of which were voted best cocktail of the year in 2012 Los Angeles. Whether I have contributed to the craft in general I am not sure, but I know I have for sure inspired fellow bartenders to try similar methods. In opening Woodson & Ford I gave a few of my staff back then a window of opportunity to learn a better and more rewarding way of making drinks and tending bar, a couple of which have gone on to become very successful NY-based bartenders. I am proud of them and glad I could give them the springboard they needed.

How do you prepare for a shift?

I like to try doing yoga before a busy shift to get my mind emptied. We also listen to cranking loud music for nine hours at work so I like to sit peacefully and read my NY Times before being assaulted by so much sound. I have a bit of OCD and so I like to straighten everything on my well and have it organized so that everything is at my fingertips when needed, kind of like a surgeon. I hate a messy bar, it irritates me. I believe everything in a customer's eye view needs to be as clean and tidy as possible or it makes you and the business look out of control and disorganized. Making sure I am hydrated.

Any particularly embarrassing moments stand out?

Mostly shakers coming apart and dumping liquid or ice all over me, has happened a couple of times in my career. A blender exploding and covering me with blackberry puree was another, that was kind of like a cartoon where I had to wipe my eyes clear.

What's the most important aspect of tending bar for you?

Making sure that the drinks are consistent, taste and look good, being a hospitable host that can keep my bar guests coming back for the love I give them as well as a fantastic product. Trying to look like I do my job effortlessly, not always easy especially when you have a high-maintenance or cranky guest at the bar.

What am I missing? What would you like to add?

As a woman am glad to see women bartenders banding together especially for causes such as Speedrack, that promote both women behind the bar and women's health issues. It's a highly competitive business and we should stick together more as sisters rather than rivals.

Hannah Lanfear, Boisdale Group, London, UK.

How long have you worked behind the bar?

13 years.

Which bars, and where are they?

Roadhouse, Utrecht; Milk & Honey, London; Mahiki, London; The Hide, London; Bungalow 8, London; Nimb, Copenhagen, and Boisdale, London.

Has being a woman helped or hindered you as your career has progressed?

I suppose both in various ways. Climbing through the ranks hasn't always been easy. Hospitality is a multicultural industry and there are guys of certain cultures who struggle to take instructions from women.

Occasionally, it's women guests themselves that will purposefully wait when you go to serve them because they doubt your skill as a female behind the bar. On the whole, though, I believe that if you put in the effort to make this your career, immerse yourself in the education of it and graft away, there's no obstacle apart from your own ambition. Women are said to have excellent taste buds, and we can often lack the bravado male instinct, meaning there are female bartenders who concentrate on making and balancing great drinks without the disability of ego.

What do you love, and what do you hate, about the way in which customers treat you, as a woman, when you are behind the bar?

Well, there is the assumption that you're not as good as the boys, and that occasionally still rears its head, I suppose because it is one of those industries where it's mostly guys, we're considered the outsiders. Usually the techniques I employ to make drinks are visibly not those of a beginner, and hopefully the drinks win them over pretty rapidly.

What I love about being behind the bar as a woman is I think what we all, as a collective, love about it, but also that there's a level of bartending unknown to the average Joe, and being able to host their foray into the world of magnificent beverages is a joy. Usually the knowledge, technique, and passion that go into it blow their minds. And blowing minds is the best!

What advice would you give to other women who want to become bartenders?

Arm yourself with knowledge, fine-tune your balance, make sure everyone is having a good time (including yourself) and certain success will be yours.

What do you think has been your greatest contribution to the craft?

You'll have to ask the people I've made drinks for and worked with. Hopefully I've made some folk have a particularly good evening out on the sauce. I have tried as a bar manager to make education a key part of what I do, hopefully I've set some kitten bartenders out on the right path.

How do you prepare for a shift?

Some old school disco and a detailed mise[-en-place]!

Any particularly embarrassing moments stand out?

I used to work in a flair bar and in making a Screaming Orgasm (I know, I know!!), I double-spun the tin to catch it behind my head. I caught it, sort of, but it was wet and pinged out of my fingers, landing over the bosom of my guest, she was soaked. I told her she could have that one on the house.

What's the most important aspect of tending bar for you?

Well I enjoy the sum of its parts. It's a very skilled job, involving so many disciplines. The key aspects that I like are building a good rapport with guests, and then enjoying the craft of building them great drinks. It's an instant gratification seeing them enjoy something you've tailored for them. But then on the other hand I enjoy a slamming dispense shift, banging out drinks in 5th gear, or a shift in a dispense bar. It's a versatile job.

If the question is what do I think is most important, I'd still say a smile. You can serve a terrible drink with a great service and the guest will still have a good time. A great drink from a surly bartender with no smile is an irretrievable experience, yet one that is still too common.

What am I missing? What would you like to add?

I'm really proud of belonging to the established little club we have in London of female bartenders. They're all such foxy winners who have contributed so much to the education of new bartenders and also to the development of killer drinks, and it's to them I'd like to raise a glass.

Jenn Tosatto, Rieger Hotel Grill and Exchange, Kansas City, MO.

How long have you worked behind the bar?

Around 10 years.

Which bars, and where are they?

Nona's Italian Café, Springfield, MO; Bar Natasha, Kansas City, MO; Firefly, Kansas City, MO; Double T's Roadhouse, Merriam, KS; Manifesto, Kansas City, MO; and Rieger Hotel Grill and Exchange, Kansas City, MO.

Has being a woman helped or hindered you as your career has progressed?

I'm actually of two minds about questions like this. One half of my brain says what does my sex matter? Why do I get "that awesome female bartender" instead of just "that awesome bartender"? But the other half of my brain says of course it matters! Being a kick-ass female is rewarding in any industry. That being said, when it comes to helping or hindering, I feel like it has been a little bit of both. When I first broke into the bar scene, more on the beer-tender, speed bartending side, it definitely helped that I was a female. The kinds of bars I was working at wanted women behind the bars because that is what the clientele preferred, and more money was made.

As I have grown as a bartender, and moved toward the craft side of bartending, I won't say that being a female has hindered me, but I think it has definitely become more of a talking point. Females are the minority in the craft bartending community, so people always want to focus on the fact that you are a woman in a male-dominated industry. In most interviews it is a question that comes up. It's only annoying when the fact that you are a woman is the focus of questioning, rather than what you are doing in the industry or what you have been doing professionally.

What do you love, and what do you hate, about the way in which customers treat you, as a woman, when you are behind the bar?

I am a total attention hog. As a Libra and a middle child, I am in a constant state of "Love me…Please love me…" But hey, I own it. It is nice to stand out among the gentlemen in vests that surround me. And being a woman in a male-dominated industry does seem to lend itself to standing out. I love the shock on an older gentleman's face when I can tell him things about his favorite whiskey that even he doesn't know. I do hate the wrong kind of attention though. I especially don't appreciate the overly flirtatious "hey sweetheart" mentality that some guests have, thinking that by flattering me I will suddenly be a blushing little thing willing to serve no one else but them.

What advice would you give to other women who want to become bartenders?

The biggest advice I have is to study your ass off, just like for any other job, and refuse to take no for an answer. Read everything industry related that you can get your hands on. If you know your craft and have a desire to keep learning, you are a much more desirable employee. My job I have now is the culmination of a year of nearly stalking Ryan Maybee until he broke down and hired me at Manifesto and the Rieger Hotel, where I could study with bartenders that I respected and knew had some big things to teach me.

What do you think has been your greatest contribution to the craft?

One of the things I am most proud of was being a part of the founding of the Kansas City chapter of the USBG. Five of us met and planned and did a ton of footwork for around six months, crossing our T's and dotting our I's before being recognized as a new chapter in August of 2012. There has been no endeavor of mine more rewarding. It is especially heartwarming to think that I was a part of starting something that will endure, and that will be a source of education, inspiration and camaraderie to future bartenders in KC long after I'm gone.

How do you prepare for a shift?

I am ready for the shift in three easy steps.
1. Make sure the Mohawk is perfectly coiffed.
2. Walk the bar and make sure everything is set for the shift.
3. Decide on one cocktail that I am going to sell the shit out of that night.

Any particularly embarrassing moments stand out?

Probably the only time any guest has ever gotten physical with me. I got punched in the face by a drunk 60-year-old woman who was mad that I had cut her off. I could not stop laughing I was so shocked.

What's the most important aspect of tending bar for you?

I can only hope that the answer to this question is universal. Hospitality and the guest's experience are paramount. We are so blessed in the service industry. People come to spend some of the highest and lowest times in their lives with us.

They come to us to celebrate graduations, to grieve after funerals. Who else gets to be a small part of such defining points in the lives of complete strangers. I take that honor very seriously, even on the normal, every-day days.

It doesn't matter if you make the world's best cocktail if no one wants to sit at your bar. I am a bit worried about the "I am a bartender so I am a rockstar and you are privileged to be served by me" mentality that I have witnessed on more than one occasion. I feel that there are a few young or misguided bartenders out there today who place ego above the guest. I have heard a bartender throw a book of random knowledge at a guest who clearly didn't care or felt like he was in class, simply because the guest mispronounced Laphroaig. It is okay to take immense pride in what you do, and you should, but never should you feel superior to those across the stick. There is a way to talk facts and share knowledge without making the guest feel alienated and like they are being constantly corrected.

What am I missing? What would you like to add?

I would just like to add that Gaz is my Boo.

Jill Saunders, Little Red Door, Paris, France.

How long have you worked behind the bar?

4 years.

Which bars, and where are they?

The Savoy and The Hoxton Pony in London. I am currently at The Little Red Door in Paris and also occasionally at Bar le Coq, Paris.

Has being a woman helped or hindered you as your career has progressed?

A bit of both in specific situations but overall I don't think it made that much difference for me either way.

What do you love, and what do you hate, about the way in which customers treat you, as a woman, when you are behind the bar?

In general, I don't think I get treated that differently to the guys I work with- maybe I should be worried, haha.

What advice would you give to other women who want to become bartenders?

This isn't really gender-specific advice but for me the hardest part of becoming a bartender was getting behind the bar in the first place. I'd worked in pubs and bars before but not cocktail bars, and usually bar managers understandably want someone who already has cocktail experience up their sleeve. Most people start their bartending careers as barbacks or servers, so do that and then just keep pestering your boss to let you go behind the bar one or two days a week, learn all the cocktail recipes and the back bar, work hard, be nice to the guests and soon you will be indispensable!

How do you prepare for a shift?

I don't really do anything in particular. I probably should though, as sometimes my natural energy is a little bit chaotic and it's always better to start a shift nice and calm.

Any particularly embarrassing moments stand out?

I have many but I will choose one that wasn't my own doing! One of the cabaret singers at the Savoy always used to try and incorporate me shaking a cocktail into her 'All That Jazz' routine as a kind of percussion and as our bar was on a stage, I didn't have much choice in it. I wouldn't have minded but she was very theatrical, with lots of jazz hands and a big, cheesy smile—I didn't want to be in her show!! I was just praying every time she performed that the guests would order stirred drinks.

What's the most important aspect of tending bar for you?

Obviously you need to be able to make a great drink, but that should be a standard minimum of any good bar anyway—

so for me it is the hosting and customer service. I nearly always sit at the bar as opposed to a table so my favourite bars are where the bartenders have great personalities and make you feel welcome. I've visited a few bars which are pretty famous but the staff have been a bit disengaged from their guests and so even if the drinks are good it really puts me off.

Karah Carmack, The Esquire Tavern, San Antonio, TX.

How long have you worked behind the bar?

8 years.

Which bars, and where are they?

Red Blood Club, Dallas; Web House, San Antonio, TX. Mostly dives up until now.... The Esquire Tavern, San Antonio.

Has being a woman helped or hindered you as your career has progressed?

I think before I established myself, my boss (and now mentor) probably didn't expect to see me go too far, he was easily angered by me in ways [that in] men would slip by. Eventually after I proved myself, [being a woman] rapidly began helping me progress, the industry here in San Antonio all of the sudden had a female that was doing what only men were doing and they all started to notice.

What do you love, and what do you hate, about the way in which customers treat you, as a woman, when you are behind the bar?

When customers realize I'm their bartender there is sometimes a series of reactions. It depends on the category of human the person falls in. Older men sometimes seem to see it as some sort of joke, and "pour me a beer, sweetie" has become the bane of my existence; younger people are much more welcoming, along with people in a couple (generally older couples, as younger women in young couples seem put off and almost jealous). I love customers who have never experienced a true cocktail bar because they leave so amazed and happy and almost always return with a group.

What advice would you give to other women who want to become bartenders?

Thick skin is key behind the bar, you are going to get hot you are going to get dirty, people are going to yell at you and demand your attention and you cannot get mad. There are going to be guys behind the bar with you, you have to be able to keep up with them or you *will* get left behind.

What do you think has been your greatest contribution to the craft?

Our local cocktail conference benefits a charity organization that repairs the hearts of children in need, and I am always willing to do whatever I can to help out with that. I also am working on bringing more charity-driven events to the bars. I think if this trend of bartenders helping the community continues and grows it will only bring more attention to our craft and people will see us as a more approachable avenue for fun.

How do you prepare for a shift?

I spend most of my day before a shift hydrating and resting, once I get to work I do not relieve my co-worker until my well is set for success, everything I need to make anything off our cocktail menu needs to be within an arm's reach. Any particularly embarrassing moments stand out? When I first started working under my mentor I'll be the first to admit I did not respect this craft as it deserved to be respected. My mentor caught me shaking a margarita then pouring it along with the ice from the shaker into a glass to be served and he (in front of several customers, one being a local chef that's quite respected) took my drink back to me and yelled at me while slamming his fists on the bar. I was so embarrassed at the time but I never made that mistake again and it really made me think about what I was doing and soon thereafter I became one of his favorite employees and friends.

What's the most important aspect of tending bar for you?

Giving everyone the best service you can give is the absolute most important thing you can do, everyone deserves a bit of a personal touch to their visit to your bar, whether it be that they are returning customers and you remember what they drink, or customers who have never had a true cocktail and you make something specifically based on a couple questions just for them, or having a nice talk about something you share in common with the guest...every guest that walks through your door could have just as easily walked through the doors of another bar and you have to treat everyone in a way that will make them happy, make them respect our craft, and keep them coming back.

What am I missing? What would you like to add?

I think just a reiteration of how important it is that females understand how labor intensive this job is and how important it is to persevere. I know how rough it can be but I also know the benefits of sticking around through thick and thin and they greatly outweigh the alternative.

Lynn House, Blackbird, Chicago, IL.

How long have you worked behind the bar?

I have worked in restaurants and bars for over 22 years...I have been full time behind the bar for the last 5 years.

Which bars, and where are they?

I worked in a bar during college, Attractions in Oxford, Ohio. When I moved to Chicago I waited tables at Honda and part-time gigged at the hotel bar in the Elms Hotel, I went on to work at Houston's for several years, I was on the floor most of the time, but would occasionally work the service bar. I left Houston's and focused on fine dining and ended up back in the bar when I took on the position of General Manager/Beverage Director for Hot Chocolate here in Chicago. I worked that position for a year, left went on to work at the Pump Room, was asked to bartend there full time. I did that, left there and went on to open the Drawing Room as one of the original master bartenders, after a year there I opened Graham Elliot as the Chief Mixologist/Beverage Director. After two years there I moved on to Blackbird, where I am currently their Chief Mixologist.

Has being a woman helped or hindered you as your career has progressed?

Both. I feel like as a woman I always have to be on point. There is very little room for error. Being a woman has made me a better bartender. In general women multitask better and have a more sensitive palate. However there are still a lot of people out there with preconceived notions about women and their role in the bar.

What do you love, and what do you hate, about the way in which customers treat you, as a woman, when you are behind the bar?

I love it when people are surprised by my gender. Lynn is a French name and the way it's spelled is the masculine version of the name, so there are people who are generally surprised when

I let them know that I am Lynn. I hate it when people call me things like "little lady" or assume that I have no idea what I am doing. That happens far less and less, but it still happens.

What advice would you give to other women who want to become bartenders?

You have to have a thick skin and never let them see you cry. There are some real cutthroat people in this business and they will bully whomever they can. You are often perceived as being weak. What you have to do is be better and stronger than they are. Educate yourself as much as possible and own who you are. No one can ever put that down.

What do you think has been your greatest contribution to the craft?

I have had a lot of younger women come up to me and say thank you and tell me that I have inspired them to pursue this career. A drink is a drink—no one is reinventing the wheel. But I have always stood strong with my sense of style, beliefs, and integrity and have hopefully showed others they can do the same.

How do you prepare for a shift?

I go in about an hour earlier than I need to just so I don't have to feel rushed. I try and not get involved in too many conversations…it's about prepping for the shift and setting myself up for success. I do a little stretching before and mentally plot the day. I always look at the book as to anticipate how the night will go—that way when the 9:30 crunch comes I am ready. I prepare my mise-en-place, have a little coffee, stock the back bar so I don't have to run during a shift, enjoy staff meal and find some silly reason to laugh.

Any particularly embarrassing moments stand out?

Never—like I said, never—let them see you cry or be weak. Even this Virgo has to admit she's not always perfect or on her best game....but I let those moments inspire me to do better the next time.

What's the most important aspect of tending bar for you?

I like bringing joy to people. I have had some amazing experiences in this business as a whole....a few months ago I had two women sit at the bar, very nice and kept to themselves. They ate and drank bottled water. They apologized for not drinking, I reassured them that my job was not to force alcohol down their throat but to ensure that they had a good time. Throughout the course of the night we talked, laughed, told jokes, I found out they were mother and daughter.

Then at the end of the night they explained their visit. Their daughter/sister unexpectedly died and they were trying to deal with her estate and find homes for her pets. They hadn't eaten in two days, were overcome with grief and just wanted to grab a bit to eat so they could be prepared for the work that was still ahead. They told me that the two hours they were at my bar they forgot everything and were able to relax for the first time in days. That is the best part of my job.

What am I missing? What would you like to add?

It's really hard at times being a female bartender. I have moments where the "boys club" is just too much to handle and I feel like a salmon swimming up-stream. However I know those moments are just moments and they are building blocks not only for me as a bartender, but for me as a person. What is amazing is the wonderful kindred-ship you see with female bartenders across the country. When we meet we know instantaneously the struggles each has had to face in their markets and we know that if you have risen to the top then you are made of true grit. Sure, competition is still there, but it is about supporting each other.

ms franky marshall, The Dead Rabbit/The Tippler, New York City.

How long have you worked behind the bar?

Hmmm... a while. I started very early on as i needed to finance my luxurious lifestyle.

Which bars, and where are they?

The Clover Club; The Monkey Bar; Wakiya, Gramercy Park Hotel; Kion Dining Lounge; M&R Bar... These were the more significant jobs i had in New York. They were all very different places with their own unique styles. I also worked at a bunch of other spots in and around the city that didn't last more than a few months.

Has being a woman helped or hindered you as your career has progressed?

Both. It's at times a double-edged sword. I know there are a few jobs that i didn't get or would not be hired for because i not a man. That said, being a woman can certainly open doors in certain scenarios. It, at times, has provided an entrée into situations where being a woman doing what we do what was much less common and somewhat of a novelty.

On the other hand, there can also be pressure to be better when you're a woman, and in the minority. I know plenty of men who are passable to competent Bartenders. If you fit that description as a woman however, some people tend to attribute that to your gender, and scrutinize your style, technique, knowledge, etc., more than they would otherwise. Furthermore, at times women are not even held to the same standards as men. Apparently, we need to exist in a whole other category, which is another problem. I've heard people say " X is one of the best *female* Bartenders around..." So, does that mean that if we ranked that person along with men she'd be just average? I'm tired of this "good for a girl" mentality. We all use the same shakers, the same spoons, the same recipes, the same booze, and should be held to the same standards.

What do you love, and what do you hate, about the way in which customers treat you, as a woman, when you are behind the bar?

Hate— I've generally been treated very well behind the bar. An annoying experience i have had is standing next to a male barback and people directing their drink orders and questions towards him rather than me.

Love—The way i can get both men and women to confide in and relate to me. Again, not sure if that's a me thing or a female thing, but i find i can coax a great deal of information out of my guests very easily, and i often do.

What advice would you give to other women who want to become bartenders?

- Be knowledgeable, hardworking, do your research, don't be afraid to ask questions.
- Be prepared for the mental and physical demands of the job.
- Try to work in different types of establishments and become well-rounded.
- Remember the bar can be a stepping stone to other great jobs with career growth potential.
- Don't feel the need to "sleep your way to the top." First of all, 'the top' is moving further and further up every day, and you might not be that impressed with the view once you get there!

What do you think has been your greatest contribution to the craft? What's the most important aspect of tending bar for you?

A very important aspect of Bartending for me is making people feel good; making them feel welcome; and making them want to come back and see me. I've travelled a lot and i dine out regularly - usually alone. I relate directly to, and appreciate the guests' experience because i am often in their place. I always try to keep that in mind when i work. I engage, enlighten (if solicited), i can opine on many topics, and try to be open to their needs—whether that is to be left alone, to have their ego stroked a bit, or to give advice.

It's quite a challenge to be a Bartender these days as there are so many different aspects and demands of job. You have to find your niche, comfort zone and recognize your forte. What i strive for is to be that all-around, versatile Bartender. One who is creative, forward thinking, knowledgeable as well as being welcoming, concerned about the guest experience, fun to be around, and who makes a good drink!

I've received many positive comments from guests over the years about how good i've made them feel when they're at my bar, about the drinks i've made them, their experience, etc. I realize this is an intangible in the sense of "making a contribution" to the craft. I do feel, however, that kind of reaction from people only helps to raise their level of respect for and understanding of what we do. If i can continue to contribute in that way, i am happy to do so.

How do you prepare for a shift?

I try to get as much rest as possible, then i shave. I often stretch as well. This work is physically taxing, and my body needs to be prepared. Depending on where i'm working (cocktail focus or high volume/rapid fire), i take advantage of my commute to get into the right frame of mind. I meditate on being positive, empathetic, and not letting people's antics get to me. I don't like to speak much during the day before work because i have to be so vocal on the job — talking to people all night, yelling over loud music, repeating myself over and over, etc. So, quiet time during the day, then once i get behind the bar, it's on!

What am I missing? What would you like to add?

While diversity is a wonderful thing, and i'm happy that the pattern of hiring only *Serious Male Bartenders* and giggly, jiggly cocktail waitresses has started to vanish,

Hiring female Bartenders for the sake of it is no answer either. They need to bring the goods, be qualified, eager, and held to the same standards as men. Otherwise we end up with women hired for the wrong reasons who are not trained properly, and that's not fair to anyone. If you can't perform well, it just sets a bad example for the rest of us who actually can handle ourselves.

Also, as women we need to be able to be ourselves, show our strengths, embrace our femininity (if we'd like to) but still be taken seriously when we're doing the job well. In the end, it's all about results and what you're bringing to the table.

Natalie Bovis, The Liquid Muse, Santa Fe, NM.

How long have you worked behind the bar?

I have worked in restaurants since I was 14 (in the 1980s). I started as a busser, and later as a server and cocktail waitress. In 1991, I went to bartending school because I was moving to

Los Angeles to be a writer and an actress—so I knew I needed a "side" job. I worked in bars, nightclubs and restaurants off-and-on until my 30s, when I became a restaurant publicist. When my passion for mixology became ignited in 2006, I started The Liquid Muse. I started bartending again in 2010, while living in Spain. So, the short answer is: I've worked in hospitality for more than two decades, and since 2006 mixology has become my passion—whether bartending, writing about it, teaching it or learning from my peers, colleagues and mentors!

Which bars, and where are they?

Most recently, I've bartended in Santa Fe, New Mexico, at Secreto Lounge and then helped develop the mixology bar at Stats Sports Bar & Nightclub. However, most of my work in mixology focuses on teaching cocktail classes, doing live events and presenting cocktail segments on TV shows, focused at educating consumers.

Has being a woman helped or hindered you as your career has progressed?

Because so much of what I do is targeted toward the female consumer, being a woman has helped me. My first two cocktail books, *Preggatinis™: Mixology for the Mom-To-Be* and *The Bubbly Bride: Your Ultimate Wedding Cocktail Guide*, are written for women at pivotal points in their lives. My third book, *Edible Cocktails: Garden to Glass Seasonal Sips*, is more general, but also appeals to women wanting to bring healthier, market-fresh fruits, herbs and homemade ingredients to their tables and cocktail glasses.

What do you love, and what do you hate, about the way in which customers treat you, as a woman, when you are behind the bar?

I hate when customers automatically direct their orders to a male co-worker instead of me—sometimes men, in particular, will assume the male barback is the one in charge merely because of his gender. I also find it pretentious when a male customer will take it upon himself to enlighten me on whiskeys or other "male" spirits. I usually just let them talk, and when they are done, I bamboozle them with knowledge and tidbits of information they did not themselves know. Then, I smile and ask what they'd like to drink next.

What advice would you give to other women who want to become bartenders?

Learn your craft. Read, study, acquaint yourself with classic cocktails and do blind tastings. If you know your stuff, it doesn't matter which gender you are. And, always conduct yourself in a classy way. Don't drink on the job. Don't go home with the customers. Earn the respect of your coworkers and your customers by being professional.

What do you think has been your greatest contribution to the craft?

My books. I'm especially proud of my latest book, *Edible Cocktails*. My goal with these books is to make mixology fun, accessible, and take away the "mystery" to making a great drink. I also love teaching classes. When non-bartenders enter the bar classroom feeling a bit intimidated but leave feeling empowered and excited, I know I've done my job.

How do you prepare for a shift?

I try to exercise during the day (yoga, for example). I drink plenty of water, eat a healthy meal. Then I primp and preen in front of the mirror for a bit. I make my homemade syrups or swing by the store for special ingredients. And, I play my favorite party music. I go into work happy and ready for a great night with a positive attitude. I try to make friends with everyone at work, from the dishwasher to the owner. I think that appreciating my coworkers and saying "thank you" to the bussers and barbacks creates good feeling and makes a business successful.

Any particularly embarrassing moments stand out?

I get a bit chatty sometimes with the customer and once poured gin into a margarita because my lips were flapping and I grabbed the wrong bottle out of the well. Doh!

What's the most important aspect of tending bar for you?

The guest. Sharing, talking, smiling, making them want to come back. I strive to be a friendly face in a comfortable setting who can cater drinks to their liking. That is what creates a regular—and those regulars sometimes become friends.

What am I missing? What would you like to add?

I love mixology and the craft of bartending. I am passionate about food, drinks, culinary culture, and all of the people who make it tick. I think hospitality is one of the most rewarding and fun fields in which to work, and running a cocktail program is the most exciting within that. I am grateful I am part of such an exciting, historic, dynamic and growing field.

Rosie Schaap, South, Brooklyn, NY.

How long have you worked behind the bar?

Nearly three at South. Previously I hadn't been on the working side of a bar in about 15 years.

Has being a woman helped or hindered you as your career has progressed?

Neither. And, like many bartenders, I have more than one career.

What do you love, and what do you hate, about the way in which customers treat you, as a woman, when you are behind the bar?

Well, I don't think customers would call a 41-year-old man "kiddo." So I'm not crazy about that. But on the whole, I deeply value my rapport with my customers, male and female, and I sense that they're a little more comfortable sharing stories from their lives with me because I'm a woman.

What advice would you give to other women who want to become bartenders?

The same advice I'd give anyone who wants to tend bar. To remember that people don't just come to bars to drink; they come to drink with people, to not be alone. So engage with them, even if it's busy, even if it's just a "How are you?" along with "what'll it be?" It's not just good manners (though those should count for something), it's also how you build a following. And, naturally, wear very comfortable shoes.

What do you think has been your greatest contribution to the craft?

I've created some recipes I really love and take pride in, but I think my perspective on the whole enterprise matters more. I hope that in my writing about bar culture, I've emphasized that where you drink, in whose company you drink, when you drink—the whole context in which drinking happens—matters as much as what you drink. I'd rather not be precious about it.

How do you prepare for a shift?

Usually I'm in a mad rush after spending the earlier part of the day writing, so I don't have any interesting rituals. And South is largely a beer and shots bar, so there's little complexity in the prep. But I normally start my shift by listening to Louis Armstrong. That gets me going.

What's the most important aspect of tending bar for you?

Well, it's not just making delicious drinks—thought that's satisfying. It's engaging with people, and creating a sense of community at the bar.

Sian Ferguson, 99 Bar and Kitchen, Aberdeen, Scotland.

How long have you worked behind the bar?

Since September 2006— six-and-a-half years now.

Name the bars where you worked, and what cities they are in.

RGU: Union, Aberdeen; Inverness Caledonian Thistle Football Club Bar, Inverness; Siberia Vodka bar, Aberdeen; Braided Fig Bar & Grill, Aberdeen; and 99 Bar & Kitchen, Aberdeen.

Has being a woman helped or hindered you as your career has progressed?

I think that generally it has helped as many of the places I have come to work have been quite male oriented and they have perhaps even employed me because I was female just to break things up a little bit. The guests respond well to a female presence too, a friendly face either behind the bar or on floor service always brightens up a venue.

There have been times however that I think it has hindered me; I have found in group situations that being in a male dominated place, I do not get the same respect that the males do, or as much input into the conversation (indeed, it's sometimes harder to gain their respect). I have definitely had issues with chefs who do not speak to me in the same way that they do the males that I work with. In this respect, it's a hindrance but certainly nothing a strong will can't overcome.

Also I find that certain assumptions are made because you're a female—for example when starting a new job I will ensure within the first shift I will take a bin out or offer to do stock, etc.—a typical 'guy' job—so that people know I'm not a girly girl nor do I expect to be treated differently from anyone else.

I have also found, working my way up the ladder, that staff are more likely to come to a female member of authority with any issues they may have and then I would pass those issues up to the manager if necessary. I would like to think that this is still the case even though I am now a General Manager.

What do you love, and what do you hate, about the way in which customers treat you, as a woman, when you are behind the bar?

Hate: I find that certain customers (male most of the time) will make a lot of crude comments when females behind the bar crush ice (using a rolling pin in a boston tin, I'm sure I don't need to draw a diagram) or when shaking cocktails. I have had many a guy say 'face me while you do that, love' or 'gonna do that a bit longer' just because our curves shake a bit when shaking cocktails. If someone is carrying some excess weight it would do same thing—do people ask them those same things because they see it as funny? No. They would be afraid to offend someone!

Love and *Hate:* We are much more likely to get tipped from guys just because we put on a bit of make-up of wear something nice behind bar. Sometimes I see it as great, easy money and sometimes I wonder why we should have to make more effort than the guys.

Love: One thing I enjoy is the rapport that we can strike with customers. Male and female customers alike seem like they are more likely to start up a conversation with female bar staff.

What advice would you give to other women who want to become bartenders?

GO FOR IT! Bartending is about the most fun you can have in a job. I think that you have to be very strong-willed and able to put up with a lot of 'guy' jokes etc. but my advice would be—give as good as you get! Show them that you can have fun and that you're not just a pretty face. It's hard work physically and mentally but also one of the most sociable, enjoyable things in the world. I feel like I come to work and get to work with friends and it's like I'm getting paid to be on a night out. Be prepared for late nights (work and play), early mornings (always a struggle) and mediocre pay, but it's fantastic fun!

Also—always listen. It doesn't matter how long you've been in the trade—there are always people you can listen to and learn from. Whether it be a customer who knows something extra about a bourbon that you then go and research more about, or a manager who has a special skill in making drinks. I have been lucky enough to work alongside many great people who have each taught me something.

Lastly—never be cocky. Never think you know everything. You may think there is only one way to do something—however the joy with cocktails is that you can play with things to a person's individual tastes!

What do you think has been your greatest contribution to the craft?

I think that becoming the GM of a thriving cocktail bar, after only a year or so of working there, when before I had never made a cocktail, is a great inspiration. I think if you work hard, have a good personality and make people want to come back to the bar again and again, the rest will come. With cocktail making, as with everything else in life, practice makes perfect—practice with a shaker, ice and water first. Practice stirring. Practice everything!

I also think that taking part in competition bartending is great—showing other people what you and your bar are doing is fun and also inspires other bar staff to get up and take part in things.

Lastly I think changing my boyfriend's opinion: four years ago, when we met, Jody would *only* drink Vodka. He was almost afraid of new flavours. Now he drinks Manhattans, Flips and Negronis as a matter of course! He now works in the same bar as I do and is largely successful when entering competitions (usually beating me, which is the definition of poetic INjustice). This, to me, is a great accomplishment. He is also now bringing out a line of bitters so hopefully that will be something that many people can enjoy! It's a testament to the cocktail, when it has the power to alter someone's entire perception.

How do you prepare for a shift?

If I'm on a morning shift, just getting out of bed on time and into the shower then walking to work is my first preparation and usually the hardest bit!

I always like to make sure that the bar is fully stocked and fully prepped, then following that, to ensure my bar staff is all ready for the shift ahead.

On quieter days ensuring cleaning is done in order to make busier shifts easier is also very important.

When I know we have a big night coming up, I try not to go out or get up to much the night before, try and relax beforehand and then of course—have a drink after we're done!!

Any particularly embarrassing moments stand out?

Without a shadow of a doubt when I knocked my own tooth out whilst shaking a cocktail. Yes, you read that correctly. I'm still not 100 percent sure how it happened. All I know is one minute I'm shaking a cocktail, I hit myself in the face with the shaker and as I turned to my colleague she looked at me with horror. The next minute, I was scrabbling to find an emergency dentist! It happened at about midnight on a Friday in December—I still managed to stay until the end and cash the tills up!

What's the most important aspect of tending bar for you?

I believe that making sure that your customer walks away feeling like they had a great time and has the desire to come back is paramount. Then you know that you've done your job correctly. I feel there can be a lot of elitist bartenders who will look down on people for what they order, but people forget we all got our 'drinking education' from somewhere. 99 percent of people start drinking beer, vodka or cider etc.—it's not a bad thing.

If people are willing to learn from you, want to sit and chat so you can share some of the knowledge you've picked up, then great. If someone wants to just grab a pint, sit in a corner, read a book and listen to their own music, then that's great, too. Each to their own. If your bar can cater to both of those types of people, you're onto a winner. By all means you can laugh after shift with the guys about the girl at the bar who asked for a mojito with no rum— but if that is what that person wants at that particular time, then that's what you give them. How would you feel if you could tell that your bartender thought you were an idiot? You wouldn't want to go back, that's for sure! I've had some pretty terrible service in bars and have never gone back. That is what bartending is—tending to that one person at a time and making them feel like you enjoyed what you just did. Remember that at all times.

Tess Posthumus, Door 74,
Amsterdam, The Netherlands.

How long have you worked behind the bar?

I've been working in the hospitality industry since the last 8 years but I've been on the payroll at Door 74 for the last 3.5

years. I started out as a waitress and the guys I worked with at the Door taught me the tricks of the trade. Especially Timo Janse stepped up as my mentor and within a year I was full-time bartending.

Which bars, and where are they?

In the beginning I worked a lot on events for Immoral Concepts, located in Breda. This was an amazing catering business from chef Dennis Sluiter and he has put a lot of trust and responsibility in me. Sometimes I was preparing all sorts of finger food, other days I was serving or tending bar. After I moved to Amsterdam, I worked at Café Stigter, Café Sarphaat and Restaurant Daalder.

Besides working at Door 74, I organize cocktail catering parties and work freelance jobs at a small bar called G&T's—really really nice place—and at a club just down the street from Door 74, called Nyx.

Has being a woman helped or hindered you as your career has progressed?

I think being a woman in a man's world has definitely helped my career. Of course there are times when being a female bartender isn't in my advantage. I do recall one occasion last year. A big whiskey brand was hosting a trip to the distillery for a handful of Dutch bartenders. The brand ambassador told me afterwards that I wasn't invited because I was a female bartender and the company wanted to focus on the manliness of the brand.

Fortunately this is a rarity and there are also times when I do get a job because I'm a woman. A real advantage of being a female bartender is when I'm competing in a cocktail competition. Normally there are only one or two other women competing and this will immediately make us more memorable. The same happens when I'm behind the bar. It's something refreshing to have a female bartender in the Amsterdam bar scene and guests will remember me more easily.

What do you love, and what do you hate, about the way in which customers treat you, as a woman, when you are behind the bar?

Let's start with the hating part and work towards the positive: It really gets on my nerves when guests ask my colleague for advice on what to drink because they assume he knows better about strong drinks. What I love about the way in which customers treat me? Everything. As I said before, many of the guests are surprised to see a female bartender at Door 74 and I mostly receive positive reactions.

What advice would you give to other women who want to become bartenders?

Just do it. We need more women in the industry and if you have the passion, why won't you?

What do you think has been your greatest contribution to the craft?

I'd like to think I'm a bit of an example for female bartenders in the Netherlands.

How do you prepare for a shift?

Holland is a biking country so every night I bike to work. During this time I listen to music and focus on having a positive state of mind. When I enter the Door, I put on my favorite song and get changed in the office. This all together will take me 20 minutes and enough me-time to get me focused and energized for the night. Everyone in Door 74 has a special song and I always put them on when we need a bit of extra positive energy.

Any particularly embarrassing moments stand out?

My most embarrassing moment behind the bar, related to being a female bartender, started out with a discussion about being a female bartender!! I had an older couple sitting at my bar and I overheard them talking about girls behind the bar.

The man thought it was too hard of a job to do for a girl and the woman disagreed with him. I got involved in the conversation and told the couple that it wasn't a hard profession as long as you have passion for what you're doing. Female bartenders could do just as much as male bartenders and I almost got a bit too feminist on them.. Not even five minutes later though, I was preparing a drink for the same couple and couldn't get a new bottle open. I needed to ask my male colleague for help and... busted!

What's the most important aspect of tending bar for you?

Mudita is a Buddhist concept, meaning a state of sympathetic joy or the happiness of another's health and success in life. For me, working in the hospitality industry is connected to this concept. As a good bartender you need to get joy out of serving people and making their night special. Being friendly is just the beginning. Sending and receiving positive energy in the bar will not only make me a much happier person but also makes the boss happy. Guests will have a good night, tip well and come back.

What am I missing? What would you like to add?

In the beginning I was a bit afraid for the possibility of having to deal with drunk, angry, big and muscled men. After doing this job for a while now, I've learned that as long as you have a good team and you know what you're doing, there is nothing to be afraid of. Women tend to have a great ability of calming angry men down before it gets out of hand.

Chapter 7

Best Blogs of the Year

You'll likely find some of the points made in the following blogs to be pretty hard-hitting, so before you read them I'd like to point out that it takes opinionated folk to open up hard-to-discuss topics, and there's no need to agree with every single point they make. Think of them as jumping off points. Opportunities to open up a dialogue. In the 1970s women didn't have to burn their bras to make a point about Women's Liberation, but that act sure as hell made everyone sit up and take notice. You gotta shout to be heard sometimes.

Just Make Me a Negroni

by Andrew Copsey

gaz sez: I found the following article on the "ATB – Ask the Bartender" Facebook page. If you enjoy some thoughtful takes on our craft, the page is well worth a "Like."

This article is written by Andrew Copsey, Consultant/Trainer at ATB Bar Consultancy in the UK. You can find his company's site here: http://www.askthebartender.co.uk/

(The title of this article refers to a cartoon on their Facebook page that depicts Robin saying, "Did you ever try an inverted Negroni made with Mezcal and White Port infused wi . . . " and Batman slapping him upside the head and screaming, "ENOUGH!")

Okay, enough from me. Over to Andrew:

The cocktail scene in this country (and indeed many others) is spreading like absolute wildfire, and we couldn't be happier. That being said, we often find that many bars (if not most) are trying to run before they have really perfected how to walk. Unfortunately some of even the most aesthetically impressive and grand/expensive drinking establishments around the globe seem to be set on a rather shaky foundation.

What we mean by this is simple, and can easily be seen in the vast majority of modern cocktail competitions: bartenders are so eager and desperate to prove themselves as 'an artist' or a 'mixologist' or just as being unique that they jump on this new-age bandwagon of trying to use the most obscure of ingredients and/or serving techniques rather than really focus on what is important: balance, a clean flavour profile, and true understanding of their products. There is absolutely no need for it, and often when drinks such as these are put into practice in bars it tends to be counter-productive, or at the very least causes an imbalance in the fight (which seems to be rife these days) of style over substance…

After all, why bother making your own vermouth for your Martinis when you just leave it in a dash bottle on your bar top? It won't matter if you are using a vintage gin that's no longer in production and use ice that comes from the heart on an ancient Eskimo fortress—you will still produce a drink with an expired product that does not taste pleasant. £15? No thanks. You can by all means use a siphon to produce Cointreau/lemon juice/egg white foam to top your 'bespoke' White Lady if you wish, but again why bother if you leave it in your fridge for days with ingredients that are bound to spoil? It also begs the question—If it ain't broke, why try and fix it?

There are plenty of unbelievably tasty drinks that 99% of bartenders have never even heard of let alone tried, all because everyone is in such a rush to jump the gun and create something new/revolutionary. The fact is, drinks were far better and bartenders seemingly more [knowledgeable] 100 years ago than they are today, which is a great shame. Yes there are far more products today and in hand more to master, but you should still start at the beginning and make sure you have it right. Understand your punches, flips, fizzes, slings, daises, smashes, etc. There is no good in making a Peach Blow 'Fish' using sake that's sat on your back bar for 6 months, yuzu from a can, and strawberries from Holland that are out of season and don't taste of anything.

Relatively simple classic drinks with FRESH and IN-SEASON ingredients will beat all your fancy infused nonsense every day of the week.

We don't have the same allowances as our cousins in the kitchen—there are not yet proper institutes for prolonged study of our craft, so it is up to the individual to take the initiative. Don't just concentrate on cocktails, you should know about wine, about Champagne, about real beer and its varying styles. Study fruit and veg and appreciate their seasons, and experiment with different spices if you wish to use them—sticking saffron in something just because it's expensive isn't good enough.

In our minds it seems that drinks are around 15 years behind the food industry in terms of customer appreciation, understanding, and the trends that seems to occur. Right now in many drinking establishments it seems we are stuck in a 'nouvelle cuisine' phase, which is not necessarily a bad thing, attention to detail is important; but when more thought and effort are put into the concept and garnish of the drink than what is actually in the glass then the whole thing falls apart. It doesn't matter how good it looks/sounds, it is about taste that we are concerned. Imagine if every bar/pub you walked into in London (or anywhere for that matter) you could order a Negroni or Old Fashioned that was on point. This is totally achievable, so why is it not happening?

Bartenders change customer perception— we are the ones driving and controlling this industry, so let's make it happen. Most customers are intimidated by cocktails and the vast array of products on offer, so by making your mixed drinks more approachable and expanding your knowledge of your other offerings you can increase your customers' awareness of the drinks world that at present is not evident to them. This is our wish for 2013.

> *gaz sez:* I LOVE *this piece. Andrew makes so many good points, and he also draws pretty much spot-on comparisons with our brothers and sisters in the kitchens. I'm pretty sure that all of this will level out eventually, but it takes someone like Andrew to point out where we are, perhaps, going wrong, and make us re-evaluate our approach to the craft.*
>
> *And try to remember this: you don't have to agree with every word in articles such as this one. In my opinion, for example, there's nothing wrong with a bartender producing his or her own vermouth, as long it's done well. The secret, I think is "do what you do well"—that is, develop your own style using strengths that you actually possess, and leave the rest to others.*

It's Time to Pay Up

by Michael Butt

> *gaz sez:* The following article is reprinted, with many thanks, from the UK magazine Imbibe (www.imbibe.com), and of course from Michael Butt, the guy who wrote the piece. Michael brings up a topic that I've never seen discussed before, and I believe it's a theme that's well worth pondering. Read on, then, and if you have anything to add, drop me a line at gaz@ardentspirits.com. Over to Michael:

Last night I partook in a small number of beverages in an establishment of both quality and repute conveniently located near to Soulshakers Towers. The drinks were delicious, the company convivial and the time passed as perfectly as it only does when you're resting against mahogany.

As I finished my allotted quota I called for the bill. The bartender, an acquaintance of mine, quoted a price that was obviously much lower than the correct amount. This put me in a difficult position, and one I find increasingly off-putting: was I expected to repay this 'generosity' with an extravagant tip?

Sasha Petraske (of Milk & Honey) once taught me that the correct response to receiving complimentary drinks is to tip to the level of the original bill. I have always thought this was a very elegant way to repay the largesse of a bar owner, while effectively giving the staff a bonus for looking after one of their personal guests.

Unfortunately in last night's case, the owner of the bar was not involved in the decision-making process. Being a long-standing customer it is possible he might have produced a bill for the same amount, but as it was I felt guilty that I was being asked to partake in what cynically could be described as a stock-to-tips switcheroo. In the end I pointedly paid an accurate estimation of the correct bill, but the great feeling I had been nurturing had evaporated.

It has always been easy for bartenders to undervalue alcohol—both the financial and physical costs involved. A hardened liver and access to under-priced alcohol on many of their drinking occasions usually leads to incorrect assumptions about both a customer's ability to maintain sobriety under an onslaught of over-strong straight-up drinks, and what their perceived value of the drinks ordered are.

And this misunderstanding leads to a decreased ability to perform one of the most important roles of the bartender—that of a salesman. Without an accurate understanding of a customer's perception of value and capacity, the ability to sell each customer the perfect number of perfectly priced drinks is lost.

This laissez-faire attitude to alcohol has other dangers, not least to the bartender, who in a culture of giving free drinks to friends and colleagues inevitably partakes in far too many shots. More insidiously, as there really is no such thing as free booze, their behaviour is always noted by some of the drier members of the financial team, and with a culture as endemic as this one, the 'free' drinks become a significant factor in the low levels of pay and respect that are afforded to many in our profession.

On any particular evening there are hundreds of promotional events, product launches and society shindigs dispensing large quantities of free alcohol, and there, more than anywhere else, the pernicious nature of free drinks is exposed. Indeed, a social anthropologist who wanted to study the base and primal nature of earlier epochs could easily start at one of these receptions. Crowds of people, all pretence at civility evaporated, pushing and jostling, clamouring for their allocation, grabbing unwanted drinks to be left hardly touched, without care or consideration for the server, the host or the brand that foots the bill.

With no value attached to the drink by the customer, soon there is none attached by the bartender, so the quality of the drink inevitably declines. With no financial interaction it is almost impossible to manage a guest's consumption of alcohol or be rewarded for quality of service, and the bartender quickly becomes just a cog in a machine, feeding the baying crowd.

It hurts me to write these words—and there have been times when sobriety would have been inescapable without the largesse of friends—but I Hate Free Drinks.

Editorial feature from Imbibe Magazine
– January/February 2013.

What Caring About What Your Drink Says About You, Says About You

by Tom Macy, Head Bartender at Clover Club, Brooklyn. Reprinted from Huffington Post, New York, 6/25/2012.

> *gaz sez:* This is a thoughtful piece about being judgmental, as a bartender and/or as a guest. Tom Macy is right about many of us thinking that we must order drinks that fit what we perceive to be our personality, and that's the main reason I usually stick to Shirley Temples when I'm out on the town. . . . Read on:

If you Google "what your drink says about you" you'll get an unending list of articles that claim to decipher what a given drink choice reveals about who you are. For example, if you drink a rum and Coke, one website declares you "don't know to try anything else" and therefore "are not very adventurous in life." Ouch. I'm no cocktail psychic, but I think they might've [gone] from A to C on that one. The sad thing is people actually buy into this stuff. Yes, your drink does say something about you—it says what kind of drink you like to drink. But most people don't see it that way.

It's truly hilarious to see the reaction from some customers, usually men, when they receive a cocktail they ordered and it doesn't look the way they hoped it would. A good example is the Clover Club cocktail, which also happens to be namesake of the bar where I work. It's a classic cocktail dating back to before Prohibition. Our version is comprised of gin, lemon juice, dry vermouth, raspberry syrup and egg white. It's completely delicious. Men skim the menu, zero in on gin and vermouth and think martini—which they know won't dim their masculine sheen—and feel it's a safe bet. Then the drink arrives. It's in a coupe glass, light pink with a layer of froth on top courtesy of the egg white, garnished with a single raspberry. You'd think I just handed them a unitard and ballet slippers and asked them for a few pirouettes. "Oh, uh, heh heh, I think you better drink this," they say, sliding it to their female companion without tasting it. "I'll just have a Macallan 18 on the rocks."

In my mind I'm thinking, I'm not impressed that you ordered a Macallan 18. But I am impressed that you're willing to spend $36 to cope with your insecurities.

The Clover Club, due to the shape of its glass, color and garnish, is what these men and their friends might dub a "gay drink." Which is not just offensive to gay men, it's also completely misguided. I know plenty of gay men who enjoy scotch on the rocks plus they're actually comfortable with their sexuality. Because really, if you can't drink a pink drink without worrying that people will think you're gay, what exactly does that say?

To me ordering a drink just to appear manly conveys far less confidence than just ordering whatever it is that you feel like drinking, if that happens to be something that some would perceive as "gay" or "girly" who cares? And if you are with someone that will judge you for what you order, why are you with them?

Of course there are exceptions. Yes, I will judge you if you order a Cosmo, but not because of the drink itself (the Cosmopolitan is a great drink), but ordering one means you watched *Sex and the City* and thought, "I'll have what they're having." Then again, if you've got the balls to order a Cosmo what do you care what I think?

By the way, my drink's an Old Fashioned, and yeah, I think that's cool.

Chapter 8

The Gazzers

In this, the third volume of my *Annual Manual for Bartenders*, I'm shouting out to a score of people who will, for their sins, receive bobbleheads of yours truly, courtesy of Pernod-Ricard USA, the grand company that has been sponsoring my Gazzer Award Show from the very beginning. Thanks guys! You know who you are.

How do I decide who is worthy of a Gazzer? Damned if I know. I just pick people who stand out in my muddled noggin. People whose names crop up over and over again, always in a good light. Some of them make major contributions to our craft. Some are the workhorses that make it easier on everyone else. All of them care a common passion for our craft, and each of them makes me proud to call myself a bartender. Thanks guys.

Without further ado, then, here's a peek at this year's Gazzer winners.

Henry Ernest Bryden Besant, 1972 – 2013.

Henry was a very special man, as many of you probably know. Londoner, bartender, bar owner, entrepreneur, visionary, tequila freak, leader, big-time soccer fan . . . I could go on for a long time. We lost him this year. He was 40 years old. Here's my letter to Henry:

Okay, Hank Besant, you don't mind if I call you Hank, do you? Ta muchly.

I well remember the first time I laid eyes on you, in some outdoor restaurant in Mexico City, 2005 if memory serves. You were sitting with Dre Masso, Andrea Montague, and various and sundry other misfits who were traveling with Julio Bermejo down to Tequila. "Mexico will change your life," Julio told us. And he was right. You changed my life, too, Hank. You really did.

Remember singing "Maybe it's because I'm a Londoner" for us in La Capilla? Remember calling me a Northern Monkey, and telling me I should counter with "Southern Fairy"? We kept that going for years, huh? Remember mooning the town of Tequila with the rest of us? What fun we had. Nice arse you had, too.

I also recall spending an hour or so with you at Norman's Coach and Horses on Greek Street in London. I'd snuck out of a buffet luncheon to grab a sneaky pint, and you, Henry Ernest Bryden Besant, noticed that I'd scarpered and you also knew exactly where to find me. What a glorious hour that was. Away from the madding crowd. Just thee and me. A Southern Fairy with his Northern Monkey pal hanging out in a real London pub. What could be sweeter?

More recently, Hank, you weaved some magic behind the scenes and got me my new job at the Dead Rabbit in New York. Don't deny it, now. Sean Muldoon told me that it was your idea that he and Jack McGarry hire me to pull six guest-shifts a year. Typical Besant, I thought, making sure that his Northern Monkey friend kept his hand in behind the stick.

And now you've gone and left us, Henry. What the fuck is that about? Oh, sure, you probably achieved more in your short time here than three or seven of us regular mortals down here on God's green earth, but still, did you have to leave us so soon?

Ours is not to know the reason why, Henry. Ours is just to miss your ugly mug, and be content with the fabulous memories you left us with. I'd say that isn't enough, Hank, but it is what it is, so I'll not complain more. Just wanted you to know that you made a fuckin' big mark with everyone you touched, Henry, and we love you dearly just for being you. Fuckin' Southern Fairy. . . .

David Wondrich

Yes, I know that he's not a bartender, and Dave would be the first to point that out, but David Wondrich has done more for our craft than anyone I can think of. And he did it his way. He's a one-off, and we're privileged to have him as a part of our community.

I'd love to be able to carry on with the myth that I think that David Wondrich is a cheap bastard, but I let that particular cat out of the bag a while back, so perhaps I'll just tell you the story of how, exactly, all that started.

This piece was written for the Museum of the American Cocktail's web site in 2005, and it marks the occasion on which I first discovered that Dave Wondrich is such a cheap bastard. Don't get me wrong, though. I love Wondrich like a brother, and I find that time spent with him is time that's always very well spent. And the fact that he's so damned cheap gives me, well, it gives me something to rag him about. And because I'm so very, very generous, I even allow Dave gets to weigh in on the subject at the end of this piece.

Bloody Marys with Wondrich, Harry's New York Bar, 2005

I'm sure that Gilles, the bartender who served Dave Wondrich and me during a recent visit to the birthplace of the Bloody Mary, makes wonderful mixtures of vodka, tomato juice, lemon juice, and various sauces and spices, but I'll probably never know for sure. Not a fan of the drink, personally. Wondrich neither. We opted for Sidecars instead. The drink was, after all, invented in the City of Lights, though nobody seems to know exactly where. At least we knew what we were doing–more than can be said of the two women from Boston who sat at the bar drinking Bellinis believing they were in the birthplace of that wonderful drink. No doubt there were people in Harry's Bar, Venice, sipping Bloody Marys, too. . . .

Originally we'd planned to seek out the best Sidecar in Paris—a somewhat formidable task—but time was tight. We were leaving to tour cognac distilleries the following morning, so we sampled the cocktail in only two bars—the Hemingway Bar at the Paris Ritz was the venue for our second round, or should I say third, fourth, and fifth rounds. Two drinks each at Harry's, and another three, or maybe four, made by Colin Fields' marvelous staff at the Ritz. (Colin Fields, the head barman at the Paris Ritz, was a guy I'd known only by email until that evening. I was happy to discover that my suspicions were correct—he's one helluva great guy, and a wonderful bartender, too.)

Personally I'd planned to take it easy, but that Wondrich guy shot down his first cocktail at Harry's as though he'd been stranded on the Alps for three weeks and a St. Bernard had just arrived. I couldn't let the lad drink his second quaff alone, now, could I? By the time we got to the Ritz we had food in our stomachs, it was late in the evening, and we didn't want to offend the staff by having only one drink after we'd traveled so far to be in such an illustrious bar. Besides, we were on a cognac trip, and someone else was picking up the tab, so what the hey. . . .

Wondrich and I tend to be pretty much whiskey freaks—he's a straight rye man whereas I usually favor bourbon—so although neither of us goes so far as to avoid cognac, this trip provided a great opportunity for us both to focus our attention on the spirit of the grape, rather than the grain. Very interesting it was, too. The French distillers really know what they're doing.

I searched my cocktail database when I arrived home from the trip, and found lots of very distinguished cocktail recipes with a cognac base. The Betsy Ross, Between the Sheets, and the Brandy Alexander, of course—stop rolling your eyes, it's a great drink if you don't kill it with too much crème de cacao. Café Brûlot is an incredible drink, too, and if you ever find yourself at Commander's Palace in the Big Easy (while visiting the museum, naturally), don't leave without sampling their version. They serve the quintessential Café Brûlot.

Even the Sazerac, one of God's greatest gifts to us mortal imbibers, originally contained cognac, but the base spirit was changed to straight rye whiskey at some point toward the end of the 1800s, perhaps a result of a shortage of cognac due to the phylloxera epidemic that decimated the vineyards of France around the same time. And then there's the Stinger, yet another wonderful, if simple, cocktail, that sips very well if it's made with good cognac and just a touch of white crème de menthe.

The Sidecar, though, remains my favorite cognac-based cocktail, and the versions we sipped at Harry's New York Bar in Paris that day slid down our throats easily, releasing a beautiful late afternoon glow that lasted throughout our trip to France—the people in the cognac industry were eager for us to sample as many bottlings as possible, and we were eager to please them. They were, after all, footing the bill.

And speaking of footing the bill, I feel it necessary to point out that Wondrich never did dip his hand into his pocket at Harry's. "I'll get these," I told him, expecting at least a little protestation, but no, Dave thanked me kindly, and reminded me to tip large. We were, after all, representing cocktailians from the U. S. of A. I'll be seeing the lad again, though, and I'll be sure to make my way to the men's room when the tab is presented next time. It's an art I've more or less perfected over the years.

Meanwhile, if you haven't had yourself a Sidecar recently, mix one up right now, and make sure you use lots of good cognac—the cocktail will be sublime, and the guys in France will be able to bring more thirsty cocktail writers to their wonderful country. Once they've recovered from our trip.

Words from Wondrich

Please allow me to clear up one small point. No, I did not make a counter-offer when Mr. Regan offered to buy the drinks at Harry's Bar. As those who know me will attest, I have NEVER bought a round of drinks in my life, nor, as long as my sinews remain strong and my nerves swift, SHALL I EVER do so in the future.

Nor do I purchase drams or mixed drinks for myself in public houses or keep any sort of spirituous or otherwise alcoholic beverage in my home. Drinking alcoholic beverages is a low, base and therefore disgusting habit, and I do not wish to subsidize those who seek to extend its sway. However, since I have been blessed by nature with an unusual capacity to absorb such beverages without outward marks or inward effects of intoxication, when I find myself in the company of some poor, benighted soul who is hell-bent on self-destruction through liquid ingestion, I consider it my moral and Christian duty to divert as many of that sad sinner's financial resources as I can from their devilish uses.

Indeed, I sacrifice myself that he or she may live: every drink a lost lamb such as Gary Regan cannot buy himself because he has spent the money it would cost on me is one less mark against his name in the Great Book of Judgment.

I'm glad we've got that straight.

The Facts

Wondrich never avoided the check at Harry's New York Bar at all. I made that up. Why? Because the story of that glorious afternoon had no kick to it. It needed a punch line. Simple as that. Dave is such a great sport, though, that he took this tiger by the tail and ran with it.

God Bless you, David Wondrich. You have a bartender's soul if ever I encountered one.

Ektoras Binikos, 2nd Floor on Clinton, New York City.

Ektoras is a true-blue bartender, and a unique artist in his own right. Go to his bar, 2nd Floor on Clinton, in New York, and see for yourself. I wrote about Ektoras in Cheers *magazine some years ago, and I think that this piece gives you*

a glimpse into this crazy man's soul. Here's what I wrote:

Sometimes it's the intricate flavors in a cocktail. Sometimes it's the color of a drink. Sometimes it's the mood you're in when you raise the glass to your lips. And sometimes, the beauty of a beverage is about symbolism and ceremony. Sometimes, not often, but sometimes, all these things come together as one, and the universe smiles down on us. Such is the case with The Marina Abramovic, a cocktail created recently by Ektoras Binikos for Marina Abramovic on the occasion of her 60th Birthday. Who is Marina Abramovic? I didn't know either.

When something or someone new is brought to my attention I try to delve a little further into the subject matter. Educate myself a little. Gain a little knowledge. I consulted authorities on the matter. I Googled Marina Abromovic. The second of "about 584,000" hits (in a very impressive .35 seconds), yielded the following from eyestorm.com: *Born in Belgrade, Yugoslavia, 1946. Marina Abramovic is a performance artist who investigates and pushes the boundaries of physical and mental potential. In her performances she has lacerated herself, flagellated herself, frozen her body on blocks of ice, taken mind- and muscle-controlling drugs that have caused her to fall unconscious, and almost died from asphyxiation while lying within a curtain of oxygen-devouring flames.* A girl after my own heart, I thought. She could have been a bartender in another universe.

And what about Ektoras Binikos? Who is he? Many of you probably know that he's the acclaimed head bartender at New York's Aureole restaurant. His cocktail recipes have gained much deserved attention over the years, and Ektoras is recognized as being a cocktailian whiz. Did you know, though, that he is also an artist? His works--go to www.ektorasbinikos.com--have been displayed at some of New York's finest and hippest galleries, and his style, though a little macabre for some, perhaps, is personal, unique, and risqué. If Ektoras' works are being viewed in a parallel universe right now, no doubt someone is saying, "he could have been a bartender." In this universe we're lucky. Here he is both.

A recent missive from this Greek-born multitalented man filled me in on his thoughts behind the drink he created for this acclaimed performance artist.

He told me that there had been a little controversy about one of the ingredients he initially chose for the drink. Not really surprising. He want to put some of Marina Abromovic's blood in there. When he was told that blood wouldn't be acceptable, even though he planned to dehydrate it first, he thought about adding her tears instead. It was a no-go. He settled on red pepper powder, and assured me that "Marina slept for seven days with the powder under her pillow so that it would absorb her aura-tic energy."

Ektoras is a real thinking man's bartender. Another ingredient of note in this drink is the 60-year-old balsamic vinegar. The event at which the drink was going to be served, after all, was to celebrate Marina's 60th birthday. And furthermore, the drink he created contains 10 ingredients. This was no accident. Ektoras explained that, for him, the number 10 represented the number one ($10 = 1 + 0 = 1$), and that the number one represents "The 1st day, the new day, day of your birth." Is this guy fascinating, or what?

People such as Lou Reed and David Byrne turned out for the black-tie event which was held at the Guggenheim—where else? —and a report of the event that appeared on artforum.com, mentioned Ektoras' creation thusly: "The Marina Abramovic, a thick blood-red drink designed for the occasion by artist Ektoras Binikos from ingredients that might have included eye of newt and toe of frog, for all we knew, though we were told it was made from sixty-year-old balsamic vinegar, bitters, kumquats, and—in place of the blood and tears Marina had desired—red pepper powder. Oh yes, and gin." Sounds as though it was well received, huh?

I regret to tell you that I haven't actually sampled the Marina Abramovic cocktail, but nevertheless I was so impressed at all of the thought that went behind this creation, and I know for sure that Ektoras is a cocktailian whiz, so I'm pretty sure that the drink is probably terrific.

The recipe appears here unedited. Just as it came to me from Ektoras. Only his words can do it justice. And I'm also including a poem that Ektoras wrote for the occasion. The man thinks of everything. I'm tempted to say that I wish there were more bartenders like Ektoras, but that would be impossible. He's one of a kind. And we're lucky enough to be around to witness his genius.

The Marina Abramovic

Created by Ektoras Binikos, head bartender, Aureole, New York.

1 1/2 oz of Miller's Gin

1/2 oz Amaro Montenegro

1/2 oz Kummel (Stock)

1/2 oz red Verjus

1/2 oz blood orange juice (preferably made from Sicilian blood oranges)

1/2 oz Yuzu juice (The frozen not salty kind)

Bitters (2 drops of Gary Regan's orange bitters & 2 drops of Angostura bitters)

2 Kumquats

1/4 oz of 60 year old balsamic vinegar

* Marina's blood (sterilized and dehydrated) just a minuscule amount of the powder form.

* or Marinas's tears.

Neither was permitted, so we substituted red pepper powder for blood.

Marina slept for seven nights with the powder under her pillow so that it would absorb her auratic energy. As everyone toasted her, a strong auratic energy vibration simultananeously connected Marina with everyone in the room.

Preparation:

1: [In] a martini shaker you add kumquats, vinegar, bitters, blood or pepper powder, verjus and you muddle well in order to extract the oils from the kumquats skin.

2: You add ice cubes and then the rest of the ingredients, and you shake very - very well (A Boston shaker is always preferable)

3: You strain and pour in to a chilled Riesling glass or a Champagne tulip. You garnish with a quarter of a blood orange piece without the skin as to resemble a scrabble of flesh. You add on top 2 extra drops of bitters preferably Regan's.

PS: The cocktail is design to open up slowly, it will taste better after 15 minutes approximately.

For Marina
by Ektoras Binikos

Sitting alone day and night beside the house with the ocean view ,
You breathe in juniper, you breathe in wild herbs ,
You reflect upon a life filled with tears of laughter,
tears of sorrow, sweat and blood.
You see the full breasted Goddess ready to burst, the Patriarch of St. Sava's Church.
You hear the distant voice of a lover at the Great Wall.
Breathing in-------- breathing out.
Sixty years of play and growing any wiser?
Blood never still, identifying and defining our limits.

Jack McGarry & Sean Muldoon, The Dead Rabbit, New York City.

Since I now work at the Dead Rabbit—I'm scheduled for a full six shifts a year—you might think that these guys are getting bobbleheads 'cos I'm sucking up to them, and I can't tell you that that's completely untrue, but in my 'umble opinion, nobody deserves a Gazzer more than these guys. Why? Because they are the real deal in the bar world. They know what it's all about, they strive for perfection, and they don't stop until they get it.

I first met Sean and Jack in Belfast when Sean asked me to go the Merchant Hotel to give a presentation, along with Dave Wondrich. I was busy, Sean didn't have much bread, and I turned him down. Six months later he was back on my back. I turned him down. A few months after that I heard from him again. "You're not going away, are you?" I asked. "No," said Sean. I went to Belfast. I met Sean, Jack, and Jack's dad—a grand lad if ever I met one. It was a fabulous trip.

When Sean and Jack asked me to be a guest bartender at the Dead Rabbit, then, I didn't hesitate. "Yes," I said. I knew that I'd end up doing it, 'cos Sean's such a bulldog, so why waste energy by refusing. I love my new job. And I love Sean and Jack, too.

Leo Robitschek, NoMad @ The NoMad and Eleven Madison Park, New York City.

Leo Robitschek is one of those guys who, no matter how many times I meet him, I seldom seem to remember his face. He and I were helping Wondrich judge a Woodford Reserve competition a couple of years ago. I introduced myself to Leo. "gaz, we've met at least half-a-dozen times before," he told me, "and it was only a few months ago when you and I chatted for over an hour at Heathrow airport." Ooops.

Leo has worked at Eleven Madison Park since 2005, and in 2011, two years after he was made Head Bartender there, his expertise and accomplishments were recognized at Tales of the Cocktail when the bar walked away with the "World's Best Restaurant Bar" award.

In that same year, Leo was also named Rising Star Mixologist by Star Chefs, and he continues to develop his creative vision both at Eleven Madison Park and at The NoMad. Leo's work was recognized in *Esquire Magazine*'s List of Best Bars of 2012, *Food and Wine*'s 50 Best Bar's in America and as a nominee for Outstanding Bar Program from the James Beard Foundation.

And now he has a gaz regan bobblehead . . .

The Mentors

From 2001 until 2007 I held a series of workshops at Painter's Tavern, Cornwall-on-Hudson, New York. The course was very rudimentary in terms of mixology simply because, although I think I'm a pretty good all-around bartender, my creativity was not up to much at all. It got better, though, after accomplished bartenders from all over the place came to take the course. It was these passionate people who taught me, and each other, how to bring the cocktailian craft into the twenty-first century. They are way above me still on the creativity front, but they did help me think outside the box a little, and without them, drinks such as DAM might never have been born (recipe at the end of this chapter).

I selected just a few of these bartenders to get Gazzers this year, and I apologize to the bartenders who aren't mentioned this time around. I know who you are. I love you one and all.

Gazzers for mentoring gaz, then, go to the following bartenders this year:

- **Jeff Grdnich, Bar Manager, The Rose, Jackson Hole, Wyoming.**
- **Philip Ward, Mayahuel, New York City.**
- **Tad Carducci, Tippling Brothers, New York City.**
- **Jim Meehan, PDT, New York City.**

The Workhorses

There's a certain group of bartenders whose names have been cropping up for years and years, and although some of them win prizes in competitions and others get hired by liquor companies to judge competitions, no matter how prominent their names become they never stray away from their passion for the craft of actually showing up for work, getting behind the bar, and plying their craft.

Once again, the list of people who fit this category could be as long as my arm, so excuse me, please, if your name isn't here. Perhaps next year . . .

This year, however, these are the people who are getting gaz bobbleheads for their sins:

- **Aisha Sharpe, New York City.**
- **Carol Donovan, Chicago, IL.**
- **Charles Hardwick, New York.**
- **Frank Caiafa, Peacock Alley at The Waldorf=Astoria and The Vault at Pfaff's, New York City.**
- **Jeffrey Morgenthaler, Clyde Common, Portland, Oregon.**
- **Joann Spiegel, Mercury Bar, New York City.**
- **Meaghan Dorman, Raines Law Room, New York City.**

Keep on tickin', guys! You're the backbones of the industry.

Chris Edwardes, Hidden Bar, Ibiza.

When we in the USA think about Brit bartenders, a few names always crop up. Salvatore Calabrese, Peter Dorelli, and Ago Perrone, all Italians, are among the list of usual suspects. Then there's Erik Lorincz, of course, head bartender at the Savoy, and a Slovak by birth. Lots of us know who Dick Bradsell is, too, and Dick is an Englishman through and through, but the name Chris Edwardes, though legendary in his home country, isn't too well known on this side of the pond. Let's rectify that right now.

This man is a star bartender in every sense of the term, and he and his wife, Amanda Blanche, are two of the loveliest people I ever did meet. I LOVE you guys.

For those of you who aren't familiar with Chris, take a look at his accomplishments and know this, one of my very favorite bar moments took place just a few years ago in London when he and I snuck out from a cocktail bash to go to the pub down the street for a pint of ale and a damned good chinwag. Here's a piece I culled from Chris' bio:

Legendary bar guru Chris Edwardes started working as a cocktail bartender at the tender age of 17 in 1975 after lying about his age. He refined his skills running various bars and restaurants around the country before returning to London in 1991 to open the Jazz Café in Camden. He then moved to the Groucho Club where he spent two and a half years as head bartender and cemented his reputation in the industry. He was then head-hunted by Oliver Peyton to open the Atlantic Bar with Dick Bradsell, which he followed by another two and a half years running the bar at the Groucho Club.

He then set up and ran the bar at Damien Hirst's iconic Pharmacy for a year before starting the GE.Club at Conran's Great Eastern Hotel. In the year 2000, he moved to Brighton with his wife to set up the much-respected celebrity haunt Blanch House, a boutique hotel with a restaurant and cocktail bar. The bar at Blanch House was nominated for Best Hotel Bar in the country five times, and won Best Bar Team and Best Cocktail Offering three times each and Best Bar. Chris also won the outstanding achievement award for Theme magazine in 2007 and then for Class Magazine in 2008. He and his wife are also both included in the 100 most influential people in the bar industry in Theme magazine for three consecutive years.

He moved to Ibiza in 2010 to set up and run what was the best cocktail bar on the island in renowned restaurant/lounge venue Aura. Then found his dream bar with his wife Amanda in the picturesque North of the island called Hidden, which is already receiving international accolades in the press. He alternates this with flying around the world to advise bars and spirit brands on their cocktail offerings and running the bars at exclusive parties and is currently designing the bars, creating the cocktail lists and training the staff at the new Ushuaia Towers in Ibiza.

Norman Bukofzer, The Ritz Carlton, New York City.

If you read Joy of Mixology then you know the story I'm about to share. Norman is a close friend, the consummate bartender, and a prankster without equal. I love you, Norman!

I first met Norman Bukofzer, bartender at New York's Ritz Carlton hotel on Central Park South, in the early 1990s, and I was immediately impressed, not only by his cocktailian skills, but also by his warm hospitality and his ability to manage the bar and the customers as though he was conducting a symphony orchestra. My only problem with Norman was that he insisted on calling me Mister Regan. Nobody gets away with that.

I pleaded with Norman to use my first name, and he always agreed to do so: "Okay Mr. Regan, I'll remember in future," he'd say with a wicked grin on his face. Eventually Norman explained that he had a reputation for remembering all of his customer's names, and that if he had to learn first names as well as surnames, his workload would be doubled, so I backed off and tried to get accustomed to my new moniker.

All would have been well with this had I not introduced Roy Finamore, who is a good friend who was also the editor of *The Joy of Mixology*, to Norman some six months later, and Mr. Finamore joined the ranks of thousands addicted to Norman's wit and his cocktailian skills. A few months later we were informed that Norman had taken to using Roy's first name at the bar, and we were livid. This called for action. We made the pilgrimage to Norman's bar.

We ordered our usual Manhattans: "Straight up. Your choice of bourbon." This is always the test we give to Norman. He always uses a different brand of whiskey, and he always knows exactly how much vermouth to use to balance whichever whiskey he chooses. Ask him how he does it and Norman just shrugs. "It's just a drink," he'll tell you. Our drinks arrived, and it was time for the confrontation.

"I hear that our friend Roy Finamore is a regular here, now."

"That's right, Mister Regan, he's here three or four times a week."

"And what do you call him, Norman?"

"I call him Roy."

"And why is that, Norman?"

He leaned over the bar until our noses almost met.

"Just to piss you off."

It had taken Norman months to set up this one glorious moment. In my opinion, I was looking into the eyes of Manhattan's best bartender.

Rosie Schaap, South, Brooklyn, NY.

Rosie is a bartender. She knows bars. Intimately. She knows what bars are all about. *She gets it.* Bars ain't about booze, they ain't about cocktails, they ain't about beer, wine, gin, or even Negronis. Bars are about people. And Rosie knows people.

You can read her work regularly in *The New York Times,* and you can read her book, *Drinking with Men,* if you want to peek inside how Rosie's mind works. You'll be impressed. Promise. Rosie makes me wish that I was unemployed and living in Brooklyn so I could spend every Tuesday across the mahogany from her, shooting the shit and watching her handle the regulars, and sipping ale all day long, with a couple of Manhattans thrown in at the end of her shift for good measure.

And here I bring to you a clipping from an interview by Molly Fischer of the *New York Observer,* just to give you a look at Rosie from another perspective.

> Ms. Schaap knows cocktails and she knows bars, but she considers the two mostly distinct. "They have almost nothing to do with each other, from my experience," she said. "I love cocktails, but most of my bar life has not been about cocktails." Ms. Christensen, her novelist friend, put her up for the Drink columnist job at the Times. The paper had asked her to try out for the job herself, but she had a better candidate in mind.
>
> "It was just sort of an instantaneous realization that it should be Rosie Schaap," Ms. Christensen told me later. "Rosie cared about drinking, as opposed to mixology," Ms. Christensen explained. She was more interested in memories, associations and context. "She was really the person in

all of New York City who was perfect to write this column."

After what Ms. Schaap called "an amazing reality-TV-show-esque audition process," the Times agreed.

DAM

Recipe by gaz regan.

Created by for MOTAC'S World Cocktail Day, 2007, New York.

In 2007, Dale DeGroff, President of the Museum of the American Cocktail, asked me to create a new drink for the Museum's celebration of World Cocktail Day, and he mandated that Laphroaig single malt scotch, a very smoky dram that can be hard to work with when creating cocktails, must be one of the ingredients. It took me the best part of a very frustrating afternoon to find the right ingredients to marry to the Laphroaig, but I must admit that I was pleased with the resultant drink. It won't be everyone's cup of tea, but it went nicely with the barbecued pulled pork with which it was paired at the celebratory dinner that year. The name, "DAM," is an acronym. The letters stand for Dale's a Motherfucker.

37.5 ml (1.25 oz) Dubonnet Rouge

15 ml (.5 oz) Pallini Limoncello

7.5 ml (.25 oz) Laphroaig 10-year-old single malt scotch

1 lemon twist, for garnish

Shake over ice and strain into a chilled wine goblet. Add the garnish.

Part 2

Bar Geekery

Here you'll find a hodge-podge of pieces written by bartenders of various hues and guises that illustrate just how diverse is our craft. I love you guys.

Chapter 9

A Tale of Longing and Fulfillment

by Tomas Estes, Cafe Pacifico, London and Sydney; La Perla Bar, London and Paris, Ambassador of the Mexican National Tequila Chamber, and creator of Ocho Tequila. [Phew!]

"When they stare at you, stare back, they're weirder than you are." I got a good laugh, a reassurance from the penciled scrawl I'd read on the signpost at an on ramp to California Highway 101. I was hitchhiking with my girlfriend up north from L. A. Usually my road took me south to Mexico. This was a new direction for me and I was feeling free, floating, unfettered, something new for me. This was circa 1965 in the sunny afternoon warmth.

We were picked up by a well-worn-in Volkswagen bus full of hippies. We got into the smoke-filled back, nice sweet, mother nature air in the van. All was peace and love and groovy music.

One of the kids lying in the back brought out from his pack a skinny, thin bottle, probably 250 or 500ml of tequila which he cracked open and passed around. He'd gotten it in Old Mexico. Everyone was smiling. There was no rush, no hassle, just the allowed opportunity to let life be, to share and be there.

I will forever remember the taste of that tequila in that setting. It was foreign, way out there, funky flavors mixed with earth and wild pungent winds blown from far away, high and low. It was thick and filled with the true heart of the maker. It was sweet and so smoothly invasive. The feeling was immediately warm, tingling and awakening. I have the imprint of that tequila in my sensory, liquid core.

This experience of being on the road, out for adventure, experiencing the counterculture, the scene on the other side of convention is what tequila was, like the weed, the music and the sex and the daring to be different. The thrill of pushing past the past and going to new exotic places, this was the essence of this happening and tequila was right there in the middle, catching its breath with a slight, sly grin.

Mexico has always held an allure, a tranced fascination for me. Going across the border from California, the land of the movie "La-la culture," Disneyland and vapid conformity to Baja California transforms me, brings me sensorially into collision with REAL LIFE. No, deodorized, sanitized, homogenization there for me. In Mexico the ganglions of the nerves of life hang in the dust and smoky air, apparent and immediate.

It is commonly said that as Mexico is, so is tequila. The two are the same in nature, in image, in identity. Tequila is Mexico. Tequila and Mexico have come a long way from the '60s era. In the unrolling there has been 'progress,' the globalization, the uniformity and mass direction of our lifestyle and our thinking.

Today there is little or no hitchhiking, the intrepid ghosts of Woody Guthrie, of Jack Kerouac and the troops of hippies are largely a thing of the past. The current conformity of our contemporary culture is well fastened in and evident to those who are aware, to those who really see. The commercialized production of many of our consumables leave them soulless and neutered.

Notwithstanding the above, despite the force of mass mindedness there are tequilas which remain, telling their story of Mexico, a tale of longing and fulfillment, of melancholy and joy, of pain and pleasure, of dying and being born. Tequila is Mexico and both are full on, right in your face, sliding into your heart, real.

Chapter 10

The Most Interesting Man in the World

by Philip Greene

You know those Dos Equis beer ads, with the swashbuckling "Most Interesting Man in the World" telling us to "Stay thirsty, my friend."? Of course, he's just a Madison Avenue creation. But for most of his life, Ernest Hemingway *was that guy*. He sure as hell stayed thirsty, for life, travel, big game hunting and fishing, running with the bulls, not to mention the odd war or two. And he stayed thirsty in a quite literal sense; in both his life and in his prose, he and his characters were not shy about bending the ol' elbow.

Writers are often drinkers, but perhaps more than any other, he often had his characters eating and drinking—be it at a café or bar, or while camping, fishing, wherever—and he described it in such rich detail, allowing the reader to almost smell and taste the scene. In a 1925 letter to his father, he wrote, "You see

I'm trying in all my stories to get the feeling of the actual life across - not to just depict life - or criticize it - but to actually make it alive. So that when you have read something by me you actually experience the thing." That includes food and drink.

Hemingway's formal education ended with high school; he'd often say he attended the university of the world. Throughout all his travels, Hemingway sought to learn from the locals, to get the flavor of the place. He once said, "Don't bother with churches, government buildings or city squares, if you want to know about a culture, spend a night in its bars." A wine enthusiast calls it *terroir*, the flavor of the region. Hemingway's descriptions and depictions gave you that additional sense, that perspective, and allowed the reader another way to become immersed in the scene.

While reading Hemingway, as a foodie and history buff, I wanted to know more about the geographical, cultural and historical context, and especially about what the characters were eating and drinking. In *The Sun Also Rises*, Jake Barnes "*went down to the bar and had a Jack Rose with George the barman.*" In *A Farewell to Arms*, Frederic Henry had a couple of Martinis, noting that he "*had never tasted anything so cool and clean. They made me feel civilized.*" The Martini had a similar effect on the characters in *Across the River and Into the Trees*, in which "*they felt them glow happily all through their upper bodies.*" In "The Strange Country," "*Roger lay back and listened to the noises that came up from the street below and read the papers and drank his drink. This was almost the best hour of the day. It was the hour he had always gone to the café alone when he had lived in Paris, to read the evening papers and have his aperitif.*" In *The Garden of Eden*, David and Catherine "*were hungry for lunch and the bottle of white wine was cold and they drank it and ate the celery remoulade and the small radishes and the home pickled mushrooms from the big glass jar. The bass was grilled and the grill marks showed on the silver skin and the butter melted on the hot plate. There was sliced lemon to press on the bass and fresh bread from the bakery and the wine cooled their tongues of the heat of the fried potatoes. It was good light, dry, cheerful unknown white wine and the restaurant was proud of it.*"

And in *For Whom the Bell Tolls*, it is the ritual of dripped absinthe that gives Robert Jordan temporary solace from the rigors of war:

> One cup of it took the place of the evening papers, of all the old evenings in cafes, of all chestnut trees that would be in bloom now in this month, of the great slow horses of the outer boulevards, of book shops, of kiosks, and of galleries, of the Parc Montsouris, of the Stade Buffalo, and of the Butte Chaumont, of the Guaranty Trust Company and the Ille de la Cite, of Foyot's old hotel, and of being able to read and relax in the evening; of all the things he had enjoyed and forgotten and that came back to him when he tasted that opaque, bitter, tongue-numbing, brain-warming, stomach-warming, idea changing liquid alchemy.

I wanted to know more about that Jack Rose, to drink a Martini and feel those same feelings, to read the evening papers with my aperitif, experience the ritual of absinthe, or taste that "cheerful unknown white wine" with a grilled sea bass, close my eyes and put myself in that scene, if only for a moment. So, I began researching and collecting the drinks he mentioned in his prose, his letters, and those found elsewhere in his life. In November, 2012, Penguin published *To Have and Have Another—A Hemingway Cocktail Companion*. It's a cocktail lovers' guide to the life and works of Hemingway, featuring 55 drinks, complete with drink histories, recipes, anecdotes, and excerpts.

I somewhat soberly note that Hemingway drank too much. His was a life full of pain, both emotional and physical, and alcohol was often his painkiller. He described Gordon's Gin as "one of the sovereign antiseptics of our time," which "can be counted on to fortify, mollify and cauterize practically all internal or external injuries." Further, "he explained the nights of drinking as a necessary counterforce to the daily bouts of writing which left him as whipped, wrung out, and empty as a used dishrag." It was a "release," "the irresponsibility that comes after the terrible responsibility of writing." Many great artists have flaws, and their muses often hasten their destruction. As the poet Edna St. Vincent Millay wrote, *"My candle burns at both ends; It will not last the night; But ah, my foes, and oh, my friends It gives a lovely light!"* So, I don't wish to celebrate Hemingway's excesses, or act as an apologist for his flaws. Rather, not wanting to throw the baby out with the branch water, so to speak, my book is meant as a celebration of his life and his writing, and the sensory aspect of his writing. And, more importantly, it will offer excerpts from Hemingway's works that will allow you to embrace the *terroir*, and taste the scene.

Here's Hemingway's uber-dry recipe, which in Across the River and Into the Trees he dubbed the "Montgomery." It's from a 1947 letter to Charles Scribner, written from his home in Cuba:

> "We have real Gordon's Gin at 50 bucks a case and real Noilly Prat and have found a way of making ice in the deep-freeze in tennis ball tubes that comes out 15 degrees below zero and with the glasses frozen too makes the coldest martini in the world. Just enough vermouth to cover the bottom of the glass, ounce 3/4 of gin, and the Spanish cocktail onions very crisp and also 15 degrees below zero when they go in the glass. This has been rugged as I said but there are better ways of sweating it out than putting your head on the wailing wall."

In a letter to his ex-wife Pauline that same year, he noted that his method "gives a pillar of ice 15 degrees below zero F. and now have glasses frozen and Spanish cocktail onions frozen. Whole drink comes out so cold you can't hold it in your hand. It sticks to the fingers." Now *that* sounds like a cold Martini. Cheers!

Philip Greene is the author of
*To Have and Have Another:
A Hemingway Cocktail Companion*, 2012.

In *To Have and Have Another*, Ernest Hemingway enthusiast and cocktail connoisseur Philip Greene delves deeper into the author's drinking habits than ever before, offering dozens of authentic recipes for drinks directly connected with the novels, history and folklore, and colorful anecdotes about the man himself. With this cocktail companion, you will be able to fully enjoy Hemingway's works beyond the limits of the imagination—pick up this book and taste how "cool and clean" and "civilized" Frederic Henry's Martini was in *A Farewell to Arms*, or sip a Bloody Mary, a drink rumored to be named by Hemingway himself!

gaz sez: *Go buy this book! Now.*

Chapter 11

Ingredient Focus: Lillet

In this year's *Annual Manual*, I'm focusing on four liquids. Two are pourable, one is solid, and the last is powdered. Really.

I turned to experts in their respective fields for the lowdown on each:

- Amanda Boccato, National Brand Ambassador for Lillet, clears up some confusion about the history of this aperitif;
- Her husband, Richard Boccato, provides an in-depth primer (how's that for a contradiction in terms?) about ice;
- Bartender extraordinaire and Canadian Jamie Boudreau gives us the bitters truth (and some outrageous cocktails); and
- The estimable Camper English—do you read his blog? If you don't, you should—shows how to make Extreme Aperol, which in turn makes one mother of a fuckin' Negroni.

Fingers optional.

gaz sez: Before we get too far into this chapter, a bit of background:

In 2012, I spent about a week on the road with the Pernod-Ricard Pioneers of Mixology *roadshow, helping to host day-long workshops in Chicago, New York, and Los Angeles.* **Stan Vadrna** *was one of the presenters—he covered a wide range of topics including his ichi-go ichi-e philosophy, how to hold a jigger with style, and a study of creative garnishes—and* **Dave Kaplan** *and* **Alex Day** *of Proprietors LLC gave a fabulous workshop on how to open a bar. Then there was* **Richie Boccato**. *The Iceman.*

I'd met Richie prior to this tour, but we didn't know each other well at all before we hung out for a week or so in late March/early April last year. Now I've gotten a handle on the guy. I got his number, so to speak. I've a strong feeling that if Richie and I spent much more time together we'd get into some very serious trouble. He's smart, funny, and he knows his stuff when it comes to ice. You'll see.

During the New York leg of the same trip, a bunch of us, Richie included, had a fabulous dinner at **Saxon + Parole**. *Richie's wife,* **Amanda Boccato**, *joined us. She's way too good for him. Enough said.*

Richie opened my eyes about ice during that tour, so I asked him to contribute a piece about same for this year's Annual Manual. *Amanda is the National Brand Ambassador for Lillet and, in the form of a flurry of emails twixt a bunch of cocktail geeks last year, she cleared up all sorts of confusing information about the product.*

Read on, and in this chapter and the next you'll meet the Boccatos, and learn about ice and Lillet. Then tuck these subjects neatly under your belt and use your new-found knowledge to further your career, and astonish your guests and your work-pals.

Here's Amanda's official bio:

Amanda V. Boccato, National Brand Ambassador for Lillet

Amanda Boccato, sometimes known as "Lady Lillet," is the sole U.S. representative for Lillet, the French Aperitif from Bordeaux (1872). As the official face of this iconic French brand, Boccato's duties include touring the country to share the story of Lillet, teach the art of aperitif and showcase the versatility of Lillet in both classic and contemporary cocktails.

Prior to joining William Grant & Sons (Hendrick's Gin, Glenfiddich, Sailor Jerry Rum), Boccato held the position of Mixologist & Brand Educator for Rémy Cointreau USA and was responsible for helping develop and execute the liqueur's trade educational cocktail program. She received her training at some of New York City's most widely recognized craft-cocktail bars, beginning at Pegu Club, where she apprenticed under the wing of mentor Audrey Saunders, and then went on to work at PDT alongside famed barman Jim Meehan.

Most recently, she has continued her tenure in having helped launch Milk & Honey outpost, Dutch Kills, with Richard Boccato and renowned proprietor Sasha Petraske in Long Island City, Queens. She has also traveled the world extensively to provide consultation and educational seminars for the spirits industry. Boccato holds a degree from the Fashion Institute of Technology and a Masters of Arts degree in Media Production from The New School in New York City.

"Lillet is a brand with idyllic character, elegance, and genuine provenance," says Boccato. "I am excited to show the world how approachable and enjoyable Lillet can be and how easy it can be to incorporate a bit of French joie de vivre in everyday life—from after-work aperitif hours, to home bars and cocktail repertoires."

"Amanda's passion for masterfully-crafted cocktails makes her the perfect addition to the William Grant & Sons family," says Laurence Costa, Lillet Brand Manager. "She has a deep appreciation for the classic cocktail canon and history of spirits, as well as a keen interest in industry innovation—all of which make her an ideal representative of the storied and iconic Lillet brand."

> *Disclaimer: Lest you are wondering, Lillet has not paid a penny for the following coverage. I picked the product for this year's Annual Manual so that, for once and for all, we all get our facts straight in regards to Lillet.*

Lillet Blanc vs. Kina Lillet

"The name's Lillet; Kina Lillet. I'm Licensed to Thrill."

Lillet Blanc is a versatile ingredient. It has no problem stepping up to the glass as a substitute for dry vermouth, it stands tall when it's chilled down way cold and served as an aperitif, and as you probably know, Lillet Blanc is an essential ingredient in the Vesper, a classic cocktail that gained fame via a spy book published in the 1950s. The following was ripped from the pages of Wikipedia:

"The drink was invented and named by fictional secret agent James Bond in the 1953 novel Casino Royale.

"'A dry martini,' [Bond] said. 'One. In a deep champagne goblet.' 'Oui, monsieur.' 'Just a moment. Three measures of Gordon's, one of vodka, half a measure of Kina Lillet. Shake it very well until it's ice-cold, then add a large thin slice of lemon peel. Got it?' 'Certainly, monsieur.' The barman seemed pleased with the idea. 'Gosh, that's certainly a drink,' said Leiter. Bond laughed. 'When I'm...er...concentrating,' he explained, 'I never have more than one drink before dinner. But I do like that one to be large and very strong and very cold and very well-made. I hate small portions of anything, particularly when they taste bad. This drink's my own invention. I'm going to patent it when I can think of a good name.' —Ian Fleming, Casino Royale.

"The novel goes on with Bond telling the barman, after taking a long sip, 'Excellent ... but if you can get a vodka made with grain instead of potatoes, you will find it still better,' and then adds in an aside, 'Mais n'enculons pas des mouches' (English: But let's not bugger flies—a vulgar French expression meaning 'let's not split hairs').

"Bond eventually calls it the Vesper, named after the novel's lead female character, Vesper Lynd. A Vesper differs from Bond's usual cocktail of choice, the martini, in that it uses both gin and vodka, Kina Lillet instead of the usual dry vermouth, and a lemon peel instead of an olive. Although there is a lot of discussion on the Vesper, it is only ordered once throughout Fleming's novels and by later books Bond is ordering regular vodka martinis, though he also drinks regular gin martinis."

Cocktailians have long debated the Kina Lillet question—what was different about Kina Lillet? Was it made according to a different formula from the Lillet Blanc that we all know and love? If so, would we perhaps never know the true nature of a Vesper cocktail? What kind of universe would let such a thing come about?

Phil Greene, legal counsel for the Museum of the American Cocktail, descendant of the Peychaud family of New Orleans, and author of *To Have and Have Another: A Hemingway*

Cocktail Companion, brought up this question on February 29, 2012 in an email sent to many illustrious cocktailian types. And me. Here's what he wrote:

> "Gents, quick Q if I may. Ian Fleming gave us the Vesper, to be made with Gordon's, vodka, and Kina Lillet. For years I've read that it's not the same as domestically available Lillet Blanc, not enuf quinine in the LB, different formula, etc. Lately, however, I hear it's not true, that it's the same product, you CAN make a legit Vesper with Lillet Blanc (ok, so maybe it's the Gordon's that's changed). Which is it? I'll hang up and listen. Thnx. Phil Greene"

Dale DeGroff was the first to respond to Phil, and although he didn't have a definitive answer, he sure as hell knew who to contact to get the skinny on this topic:

> "[some] blogs claim that Suze and Cocchi Aperitivo Americano is a good sub for the original Lillet ... I don't know if that is true. I copied Amanda Boccato she is the Lillet ambassador and may have the answer."

And Amanda came to the rescue. As did **Ted "Dr. Cocktail" Haigh**. We'll listen to Doc first:

> "In 1986 Bruno Borie, principal of Château Ducru-Beaucaillou, swept up the Kina Lillet company in the great trough of its popularity. Would Kina Lillet have met its demise without the hand of Borie? Perhaps not, but it was Borie's hand that made it catnip for multinationals like Diageo's precursors and Pernod Ricard.
>
> "When Borie acquired the brand, he set about to extend the reach of both its marketing and distribution. Part of doing so was a streamlining of the brand in both formula and name. Lillet is more memorable than Kina Lillet unless its main clientele had substantial foreknowledge. By and large, it did not."

So now we know that 1986 was a pivotal year for Kina Lillet, but was this the year in which the quinine content got significantly diminished in the formula? Nope. Fact is, according to Amanda, the Lillet Blanc we drink today is pretty much the same Lillet that's been on the shelves since the late 1800s. So how come we've been thinking otherwise?

The misinformation seems to have stemmed from an article written by Toby Cecchini in *The New York Times*, but Amanda is quick to point out that Toby was not responsible for this—

he was simply given some facts that turned out to be fantasy. Here's what she had to say on this issue:

> "Within the article, were at least three pieces of information that were plainly incorrect, likely because the information wasn't readily obtainable. I might add that the article was written by a friend and a respected peer . . . I believe the brand, in the past, is to blame for not getting the information out there readily, not the writer of the article (of course). In a nut shell, that's why they hired me— to bring the correct information to the people! Good move, Lillet! Thanks for the gig—how swell!"

Phew! I pretty much idolize Toby Cecchini and, despite him being an arrogant, over-educated type, he's a good friend, and I always think that he and a certain Mr. Wondrich are probably the best wordsmiths in the booze-writing business. Fact is, if Toby spilled incorrect information, it's because he was given incorrect information by a source that he believed to be reliable. So what were the three pieces of incorrect information within Toby's article? Over to Amanda again (the following has been lightly edited):

Incorrect

1. Quinine was taken out of Lillet when the word "Kina" was dropped from the title.
2. Lillet is a digestif.
3. Lillet has additional herbal additives aside from quinine.

Correct

1. The word "Kina" was taken out of Lillet because of what I can only refer to as "marketing relevance." Before the 80s, the fact that the product alluded to the quinine that is in it was relevant to marketing the product simply because of "the times." It was a helpful push for the product to put the word Kina right in the title because of the malaria problem. I imagine drinkers of Lillet drank it very much in part because of the remedies the "Kina" offered.

However, in the '80s, with the malaria problem losing contemporary relevance (of course this is arguable, for third world countries), taking the word "Kina" out of the title and simply keeping the family name "Lillet" seemed like the right thing to do.

Quinine is still found in Lillet. It is the sole herb in the product. Incidentally, quinine has always been in Lillet and not in varying amounts throughout the years. Like any good and loved product, they've tried to keep it as consistent as possible.

Quinine is a necessary ingredient for Lillet because the bitterness it brings forth aides in "keeping the [softer fruit] flavors in your mouth."

Perhaps today (especially from a purest perspective by those who have seen "Kina Lillet" as the ingredient in old recipe books), we might think that this change in title was quite possibly was the stupidest thing the brand owners could have done. I am starting to believe that myself a little bit each day! It's the same Lillet we have always known, still with quinine, always with just quinine as the sole herb, always an aperitif and always what the Vesper, Corpse Reviver #2, etc. call for.

2. Lillet is an aperitif, which I'm sure you all know, and always has been intended to be a "palate opener" before a meal. It has never been a digestif, or even marketed as one, as stated in the NY Times article.

3. Quinine is the only herb in Lillet, but it also contains a 15% maceration of 10 to 12 "mysterious" fruits—namely both bitter and sweet oranges, similar to say a Cointreau or Combier—and wine (85% Bordeaux blend, depending on which bottling we're talking about, the other wines can be Semillion, Sauvignon Blanc, Cabernet, Merlot, etc.).

Summation

Lillet Blanc is the same product now as it's always been. If you see a recipe that calls for Kina Lillet, just use Lillet. It's licensed to thrill.

Solid Info on this Liquid Treasure

The information you're about to encounter comes from the good folk at Lillet. Catch their web site at www.lillet.com:

The company Lillet Frères was established in 1872 by wine merchants Paul and Raymond Lillet in Podensac, France in the Bordeaux Region. Today every stage of production takes place at the Lillet distillery and has remained consistent throughout the years, evolving only slightly to reflect oenological advancements and technical improvements. The secret ingredients are unchanged and the proprietary recipe is closely guarded by the cellar master, ensuring Lillet's iconic status as the Quintessential Aperitif of Bordeaux.

Lillet Blanc

The wine used for the creation of Lillet Blanc is sourced from the best Entre Deux Mers grapes. The wine used is the result of the careful blending of different grape variety like Semillon, for its structure and long finish, Sauvignon Blanc, for its fruitiness and aroma, and muscatel for its floral bouquet and elegance. During the aging process, the lees are stirred back into the wine which gives Lillet's fat consistency.

The wine is then married with fine artisanal orange liqueur crafted from sweet orange peels from Spain and bitter oranges from Haiti. Cold macerated in 48% neutral alcohol, the "vinage" also consists of the addition of a secret blend of 10 fruit liqueurs. The fine liqueurs used are produced in Lillet's distillery in Podensac, in the same time honored manner since the early 19th century. A small amount of quinine from Peru is added to the blend before the liquid is aged 6 to 12 months in French oak barrels, the wood for which is sourced from the forests of Tronçais in central France. To achieve perfect consistent balance, the master distiller blends young vintages of Lillet, fresh and fruit forward, with smoother more concentrated older vintages. He then proceeds to a final "assemblage" making careful adjustments for quality before it is bottled

Varietal Composition: 80% Semillon, 15 % Sauvignon Blanc, 5 % Muscadel

Fruit Liqueurs: 85% Orange liqueur, 15% [other] Fruit liqueurs

Production Facility: Podensac, Bordeaux

Aging: 6 to 12 months in French oak barrels : 22,000

Alcohol Content: 17% vol.

Appearance: Brilliant, Shimmering, Gold Color

Nose: Honeysuckle, Orange Blossom, Lime, Fresh Mint, Vanilla

Taste: Fresh, bold and fruity with balanced structure and length on the palate

Awards: 95 Points - Highly Recommended – Superb, Wine Enthusiast, August 2009;

Silver Medal, 2009 San Francisco World Spirits Competition.

Lillet Rouge

The wine used for the creation of Lillet Rouge is sourced from terroirs which produce fine Merlots & Cabernet Sauvignon, including Haut Medoc, prized for their full-bodied and peppery qualities. The wine used is the result of the careful blending of Merlot, Cabernet Sauvignon and Cabernet Franc.

The wine is then married with fine artisanal orange liqueur crafted from sweet orange peels from Spain and bitter oranges from Haiti. Cold macerated in 48% neutral alcohol, the "vinage" also consists of the addition of a secret blend of 10 fruit liqueurs, produced in Lillet's distillery in Podensac, using the same time-honored manner since the late 19th century. A small amount of quinine from Peru is added to the blend before the liquid is aged 6 to 12 months in French oak barrels, the wood for which is sourced from the forests of Tronçais in central France. To achieve perfect consistent balance, the master distiller blends young vintages of Lillet, fresh and fruit forward, with smoother more concentrated older vintages, and then proceeds to a final "assemblage" making careful adjustments for quality before it is bottled.

Varietal Composition: 80% Merlot, 15% Cabernet Sauvignon, 5% Cabernet Franc

Fruit Liqueurs: 85% Orange liqueur, 15% [other] Fruit liqueurs

Production Facility: Podensac, Bordeaux

Aging: 6 to 12 months in French oak barrels

Alcohol Content: 17% vol.

Tasting Notes: "Cherry-red color. Assertive bouquet of freshly picked grapes, black cherries, black raspberries, apricots and pepper keeps the olfactory sense focused. In the mouth, it behaves like a fat, chewy red from the sun-drenched south of France; tastes ambrosial and clean." Wine Enthusiast, August, 2009

Awards: 89 Points -Recommended – Very Good, Wine Enthusiast, August 2009.

Lillet Rosé

Since 1872, Lillet has been crafted in Podensac, a picturesque village in Southwestern France. In 1962, Lillet introduced Lillet Rouge, its first new product in over 50 years. Now, Maison Lillet presents its first offering since that time – Lillet Rosé.

Created from the same classic Grand Cru Bordeaux wine varietals as Lillet Blanc and Lillet Rouge, Lillet Rosé's uniqueness is marked by the addition of new fruit liqueurs produced with Maison Lillet's secret recipes. The customary quinine is added, and the result is a lush, fruity, elegant tonic wine perfect for enhancing warm summer evenings and more.

Lillet Rosé is characterized by ripe summer berries, wildflowers, melon, and stone fruit, as well as the traditional sweet and bitter citrus notes.

Tasting Notes: "Inviting aromas of fresh flowers, ripe berries and spring garden abound. Flavor profile highlights the fruity-grapy-berry element to glorious result; irresistibly luscious." Paul Pacult, 2011 Ultimate Beverage Challenge

Awards: Chairman's Trophy (94 Points / Excellent, Highly Recommended / Good Value) 2011 Ultimate Beverage Challenge;

Gold Medal, 2011 San Francisco World Spirits Competition,

Chapter 12

Ingredient Focus: Ice

The Cold War (or How I Learned to Stop Worrying and Love the Ice)

> *gaz sez: In the 2011 Annual Manual, I talked a little about ice and water as an integral part of cocktails. But I realized there's a lot more to learn about ice, so I asked Richard Boccato to explain some of the science. If anyone knows more about ice than Richard Boccato, I've yet to meet them.*

Here's Richie's official bio:

> Richard Boccato was born in Florence, Italy, and raised in Brooklyn, New York. From 2005-2009 he was employed as a bartender at Little Branch and Milk & Honey, respectively. In May of 2009, Boccato and Sasha Petraske swung the doors of Dutch Kills, a cocktail saloon in Long Island City, Queens, where block ice has been hand-cut down to size for cocktails directly behind the bar since day one. In the zpring of 2010, Boccato opened PKNY aka "Painkiller", a New York City Tiki Bar. In December, 2010, Boccato teamed up with Brooklyn's finest cocktail crew to open Weather Up Tribeca in downtown Manhattan, which is the first bar in the

world to feature in-house block ice production with its own Clinebell CB300X2D carving block ice making machine, yielding 600 pounds of crystal-clear ice every two-to-three day cycle. In the spring of 2011, Boccato and his Dutch Kills colleagues chose to further their Clinebell fascination when they brought forth Hundredweight, a block ice production and delivery service for cocktail bars and beyond. In May of 2012, Boccato and his Weather Up partners expanded their horizons to Austin, Texas, to include a new cocktail bar and block ice production facility.

See what I mean? Now, over to Richard:

The Cold, Hard Facts

This is not an article about the historical and cultural developments that prompted mankind to harvest and harness frozen water for use in alcoholic beverages, nor is this article intended to sway allegiance toward a block ice program in every cocktail bar the world over. This article is most assuredly not intended to expressly disparage the commercial ice making industry, nor is it intended to challenge or besmirch any of the hypotheses and cocktail ice experimentation conducted by others.

These words were commissioned for the sole purpose of illustrating and exploring the merits of but one method in a million by which we all can achieve excellence in the preparation and service of the modern cocktail. So let's get on with it.

Most bartenders and all other interested parties should by now be in full accordance that aside from effortless grace, affable wit, and a winsome smile, the three predominant factors that govern the execution and outcome of a superior and successful cocktail behind the modern bar are (in no particular order):

1. Balance:

This is accomplished solely by the bartender—who is (hopefully) taking pains to carefully measure out each and every component of each and every cocktail that passes over their bar. A minuscule discrepancy of a single ingredient in either direction will indeed make a discernible difference between the real turtle soup and the mock.

2. Temperature:

There are several mitigating factors at play here, such as…
1. Ambient temperature in the bar.
2. Does the bartender keep glassware in the freezer (most should)?
3. Does the bartender keep booze in the freezer (some actually do)?
4. Does the bartender keep service ice in the freezer, or is it merely sweating away in the confines of a room-temperature ice bin at zero degrees Celsius?
5. What specific variety and gradation of ice is the bartender using to execute cocktails?

3. Water Content, or ABV% of a cocktail:

Arguably, there is already water content inherent in the ingredients of every cocktail prior to these components being combined with ice (e.g. citrus, modifying agents in the form of sugar or liqueurs, the stated ABV% of the base spirit(s), added carbonation, etc.). However, the last word on water content in a mixed drink is directly related to the ice that is being used to shake it, stir it, or occupy the glass that houses said cocktail for the duration of its life before it is willingly absorbed into your body in exchange for top dollar.

Therefore, we calculate the ABV% of a completed cocktail by dividing the total amount of ethyl alcohol by the final volume.

For example:

In order to calculate the ABV% of a shaken Daiquiri made with 2 oz. of 80-proof rum and a final volume of 4.5 oz. in a 5.5 oz. capacity glass, the formula would be .8/4.5 = 17% ABV.

It is common to hear people say that a well-made cocktail should be comprised of approximately 75% ingredients and 25% water melted from ice, but we should be careful not to over-generalize and state for the record that every bartender on Earth should be confined to such stringent universalisms. Of course we need to be concerned with getting identical results every time with certain cocktails, however these numbers should not be arbitrarily designated across the board.

It is therefore imperative that the working bartender exercises care and precision on all fronts in order to consistently hit the correct ABV, temperature mark, and washline for every paying customer without leaving an unwarranted amount of liquid in the shaker or mixing glass to be discretely thrown down the drain when the boss isn't looking. By "washline," we are of course referring to the embodiment of an appropriately stirred or shaken cocktail in its vessel. This is literally the boundary where the liquid portion of a cocktail ends along the wall of a glass, leaving a small window of space to separate the drink from the rim. By now we should all have formulated some preconceived yet generally accordant opinions on what a proper washline should look like. A glass served over the bar full to the brim way past the window and sporting a convex meniscus with heavy surface tension is generally not a good indication of the aforementioned.

Nature vs. Nurture

Ice crystals form in any body of water at what is called a nucleation point, which is a piece of foreign matter around which an ice crystal builds—usually an impurity floating about the water somewhere. In the example of a lake or a pond (which tend to freeze from the outside in), nucleation points are on the shore where the water is not as deep, and the initial ice crystals generally aggregate in non-linear formations across the surface of the water.

Clear ice from a lake is usually an indicator of a slow freezing process. As the ice crystals form, the lattice of crystals becomes so tight that there isn't any room for impurities to make their way inside, hence the reason why the slow-freezing process forces all impurities such as air and minerals to be pushed away, trapping them in the remaining portion of the ice to achieve a solid state.

As water in a lake or a pond freezes from the top down, oxygen bubbles and impurities remain unfrozen together at the bottom. As the ice thickens, the water below in turn becomes ice at a slower rate due to the fact that ice is a poor conductor of heat. The thicker the ice becomes, the further the distance the latent heat that is released during the process of freezing has to travel to reach the cold air above the pond. In essence—the thicker the ice, the slower the rate of freezing (and melting!). By "latent heat," we are of course talking about the amount of energy that is required for water to change state.

Unlike slow-frozen lake ice, most home-frozen ice cubes ice cubes develop a cloudy center because the water is freezing on all four sides of the vessel from the outside in and from the top down, trapping air bubbles and impurities in the middle. When the last bit of water on the inside of the cube turns to ice, small fissures and striations will develop and branch outward from the core, creating countless miniature fault lines. The impurities and oxygen bubbles then attempt to forcibly push their way out from the core as this water expands during the freezing process, lending the cube an overall "fuzzy" aspect. In turn, an ice cube also melts from the outside in, so its center is the last part to go bye-bye. Niceties and etiquette aside, these unsightly floaters are actually the historical rationale for discarding a guest's ice cubes upon fixing them a fresh cocktail. It is said that the American poet Anne Sexton once referred to the mineral-laden cores of ice cube remnants in a spent cocktail as "senile."

Water and ice can both coexist at zero degrees Celsius, but believe it or not, it takes a large amount of energy to convert solid ice to a liquid state. And for our purposes, this tells us that under the right conditions, the chilling properties of ice are ideal for bringing down the temperature of our cocktails without adding too much water. After all, what we are aiming to do is to make better cocktails all around, and not just "colder" or with "less dilution." Keep in mind that the smaller the ice cube, the greater the surface area, and the more likely it is that latent heat will be thinly distributed. Conversely, "big" ice cubes have less surface area per gram than smaller pieces of ice.

And since most bars store their service ice in open-air room-temperature bins, this ice for the most part remains at a constant zero degrees Celsius with water on its surface. We call this "sweaty ice" and we choose not to make our shaken and stirred cocktails with it because we know that "sweaty ice" will inherently add unwanted water content to a cocktail straightaway, compromising our ability to ensure proper balance, temperature, water content, and organically achieved washlines. We have also recognized that smaller pieces of ice melt faster than larger pieces of ice, hence the advantage of making cocktails with "big ice" that is stored in a freezer as opposed to smaller, "sweaty" ice cubes left out in the open air. As working bartenders operating within the confines of a live barroom situation, we must always remember to be very concerned with the overall water content of our cocktails, and the proper washlines on our glassware must be met in tandem with an optimal temperature for our cocktails.

The temperature of ice cubes makes a difference—colder cubes chill faster. And the size of cubes makes a difference—bigger cubes melt slower. We also know that as a drink sits on the bar top, it absorbs heat from its surroundings, causing the ice to melt. So we have come to the conclusion that an Old

Fashioned at Dutch Kills served over a piece of Hundredweight big ice straight out of the freezer with its large volume and low surface area will melt slower than the same drink served over a handful of wet ice cubes. We implore you to arrive at your own conclusions based on the particular variables that govern your environment(s).

On Stirring

If one stirs a cocktail with smaller format commercial machine-made ice versus larger format ice derived from a block and both styles of ice are kept in the freezer at the same temperature with the same temperature mixing glass, then both cocktails will likely reach the same temperature upon execution. However, we have observed with a great deal of regularity that smaller pieces or shards of ice will melt faster than larger cubes, and therefore stirring time would have to be adjusted between the drink that is stirred with smaller ice versus the drink that is stirred with only larger ice. For practical purposes when stirring we have therefore come to use shards of what we call "cracked ice" straight from the freezer in both larger and smaller gradations that serve to alternately chill the cocktail and assist in providing the desired water content at the same time. The bottom line is that our goal is to serve a drink at the right temperature with the proper washline. These desired outcomes need not be mutually exclusive!

The starting temperature of the ice that we use to make our drinks is undoubtedly the most important factor here. It is paramount to effectively achieving a cold cocktail. This is why we keep the ice that we employ during service in our freezers behind the bar (along with our glassware). What specifically matters is that this ice is dry. Any surface melt or "sweat" on ice that is introduced into a shaker tin or a mixing glass immediately contributes to the overall water content at a much faster rate than desired. The majority of the energy and temperature transfer in this process comes at the point of phase change, when the ice becomes water. There is some transfer of heat aside from the actual melting of the ice, but not much. Other factors are also in play here, such as the ambient temperature of the bar, etc. I will reiterate here that our primary concern as actual bartenders serving potable cocktails within the confines of our specific working environment(s) must remain that we are putting forth the coldest and most balanced drinks possible with the most appropriate water content and washlines for our glassware.

Even though we are clearly concerned with the size(s) of the ice in our shakers and our mixing glasses, it very well may be that having an adequately cold freezer to replace a room temperature ice well is more important than the size of the ice itself. We are constantly aiming for a colder cocktail straight off the bat, and this is why we keep all of our varieties of ice to be used for various purposes in our service freezers, along with our mixing glasses and the majority of our glassware. Admittedly, the temperatures of our freezers are compromised and raised every time that they are opened and exposed to the ambient temperature in the room during a busy shift behind the bar. That's why we don't leave them wide open all night. So we do the best that we can, given the limitations of our working environment. Key phrase: WORKING ENVIRONMENT. No matter what kind of ice you're using, the moment that you marry that ice with the ingredients in your shaker or mixing glass, the fuse on that cocktail is lit and the game's afoot. There can be no fussing about. It's time to get down to business. All differences aside, at this point our communal directive as bartenders the world over is to provide exemplary hospitality and cold and delicious drinks to our guests. This can only be achieved with any modicum of regularity by working deftly and swiftly within the parameters of the order of operations under which we abide every night behind the bar.

Giving Everyone and Everything a Fair Shake

All other things being equal (temperature of ice, temperature of ingredients, etc.), the advantage to shaking with a bigger colder single cube is that you can ideally shake it longer, thus giving you the desired consistency of ice crystals and "liveliness" that you want on the head of a shaken straight up cocktail. With that in mind, we must recall how Harry Craddock did so eloquently instruct us 83 years ago to enjoy our drinks while they're smiling at us!

Of course, the big cube must deteriorate to a certain degree in the shaker at some point during or towards the end of the shake for this to work. If you're just standing there uninspired going "thukka-thukka-thukka" back and forth without using any elbow grease whatsoever, then the cocktail in question certainly won't be cold enough, nor will it present an acceptable head when strained into the glass. Clearly it takes a more calculated effort to make the gravy with the big ice than it does to conjure several vigorous and theatrical shakes with machine ice—and in most cases with the latter you're usually holding a really cold yet unbalanced slushie in your shaker by the time you're through. For the record: shaking a cocktail whilst engaging in exaggerated theatrical gestures and gregarious displays of unbridled voracity may look impressive to your customers, however it does not necessarily yield an acceptable drink. The blonde with the poodle doesn't like to see liquid leftovers in a bartender's shaker any more than she likes to see them in a mixing glass. Both instances cause her to feel ripped off, and unimportant.

Why Size Really Does Matter

As for the proverbial Old Fashioned, building two of the same side by side using 4-6 sweaty machine ice cubes versus one freezer-stored "big" cube is probably the strongest argument toward the apparent benefits of "big" ice, whether it be derived from a large block or otherwise. This here is the true litmus test. Since we are assuming that these two Old Fashioned cocktails are not being stirred with ice in mixing glasses and they are being prepared directly in a room-temperature glass with room-temperature ingredients—then the relationship between the surface area of the ice, the temperature of the ice, the size of the glass, and the liquid volume of the cocktail itself prior to the addition of ice will be the true tale of the tape. My money is on the big ice, every time. Washlines aside for a moment, we know this much to be true: ice cubes, regardless of their size, density, or mineral content (based on initial water quality and subsequent filtration techniques) will continue to cool a drink until they are completely gone. The heat removed from the liquid in the cocktail is applied towards melting the ice, causing the water molecules at their surface to vibrate and break free of the tight lattice of the ice molecule—sending them floating away to become a part of the next sip. In the final analysis, the big ice coming out of the freezer is going to melt slower and chill the drink longer than the smaller sweaty ice. Aside from balance, these are the main results that we are aiming to achieve in our Old Fashioned-style cocktails served down on the rock.

Although I have purposely chosen not to divulge the intricacies of our specific ice production methods at Hundredweight and Dutch Kills in these pages, please understand that we go through all of this trouble because we believe in the process and we stand behind the final product. A block ice program (in-house with a block ice maker, in-house via non-mechanized block production, outsourced, or otherwise) provides a bar and its staff with a vested interest and a true sense of ownership over their ice, as well as the potential for greater ultimate control over the factors that contribute to a better cocktail. Does a block ice program require a much more labor-intensive approach to one's overall service plan? Yes indeed. Are safety and insurance coverage important factors to be considered here? Hell yes they are. Have most professional bartenders working in 2013 more or less accepted that a labor-intensive and no-nonsense approach to every aspect of service should by now be the industry standard (fresh squeezed juice, house-made syrups, premium spirits, etc.)? 'Nuff said.

As bartenders, we ply our trade by conjuring and perpetuating different manifestations of the same bittered slings that were first realized in these United States over two centuries ago. But let's get past that for a moment to understand that by introducing this particular style of frozen water into the modern interpretation of a bittered sling we are honoring the entire scope of our cocktail pantheon and reaffirming our dedication to making these drinks better by all means necessary. When we serve our Old Fashioned at Dutch Kills on a big Hundred-weight cube in all its glacial and pellucid glory, the only person who doth ever protest is the occasional Doubting Thomas who thinks that he's somehow getting "short changed" on his booze count by the size and girth of the ice in his drink. And that's when we explain to him that this isn't necessarily about merely showcasing the ice. Sure, it's big and beautiful—and material objects that are presented to consumers as being opulent and desirable invariably become highly coveted. Lest we forget that we do all of this with the ultimate intention of making hard working people part with their coin to savor and appreciate our liquid wares at their leisure. So therefore we must respect every single ingredient that goes into our cocktails. We must expect them all to stand up and deliver a harmonious integration of balance, temperature, and water content. And it goes without saying that we will never put forth a warm and unbalanced cocktail, nor will we ever serve one that is unnecessarily watery—even if it is colder than a witch's tit in December.

© R. Boccato, 2013.

Chapter 13

Ingredients Focus: Bitters

gaz sez: *Bitters, as you probably already know, have gotten way out of control over the past few years, with more and more bottlings appearing on the market at a ferocious rate of knots. Will this ever end? Yes and no, I think. Inferior bottlings and those from companies without a good marketing plan and/or budget are bound to die out sooner or later, but there are some newcomers getting in on the act, too, so I think that we'll keep seeing new bitters on the shelves for a few more years to come.*

The increase in the numbers of different flavors of bitters, in my 'umble opinion, is both a good thing and a bad thing. It's good because it gives bartenders a chance to differentiate our new creations, and it's bad because it means that, in some cases, nobody can recreate our new drinks. And yes, I understand that being the only bar in town to serve a specific new drink can attract customers, but what about the poor folk who live elsewhere?

With that issue out of the way and no real conclusions made, I'll go on to the phenomenon that I really want to highlight this year. It's been going on for quite some time, and I think I'm right in saying that a certain **Jamie Boudreau**, the Canadian Maestro who holds forth from Cannon, his own joint in Seattle (where **Murray "The Flash" Stenson** also works), is probably responsible for starting the trend of using bitters by the ounce, rather than by the drop or dash, in his new creations.

Jamie's fascination with this concept seems to have started in 2008, when he posted the following in his blog (https://spiritsandcocktails.wordpress.com):

> Mixology Monday, hosted by Joe and Dinah over at Bibulo. us, has finally dragged me to the keyboard with an interesting theme this time: Nineteenth Century Cocktails. Combing through my sources and finding a lot of plagiarism between authors as well as an awful lot of bizarre (and not in the good way) concoctions, sometimes with ingredients that are now defunct, I began to worry that it would be next to impossible to find a unique entry that would also be palatable. Then I came across Leo Engel's 1878 opus, American and Other Drinks.
>
> While my eyes flitted over such concoctions as the Flip Flap, Heap of Comfort, the Magnolia (a la Simons) and the Square Meal (which could've been substituted for one, what with the two egg yolks and salt and pepper before we even get to the boozy ingredients), it was the Alabazam (it should really have an exclamation point after the name, shouldn't it?) that intrigued me enough to actually waste good booze on a trial run.
>
> Leo Engel, an expat by way of New York, came up with the following libation while tending bar at the Criterion's American Bar:

ALABAZAM

Use tumbler.

One tea-spoonful of Angostura bitters; two tea-spoonfuls of orange curaçoa; one tea-spoonful of white sugar; one tea-spoonful of lemon juice; half a wine glass of brandy. Shake up well with fine ice and strain in a claret glass. This was converted (by me) to:

ALABAZAM

1 1/2 oz Cognac

2 tea-spoons Cointreau

1 tea-spoon Angostura

1 tea-spoon sugar

1 tea-spoon lemon juice

stir all until sugar has dissolved

add ice, stir and strain into a chilled cocktail glass

marvel at the spiciness!

The Criterion is a restaurant which still exists in London's Piccadilly Circus to this day, although I suspect in a much smaller format as this celebrated bon-vivant's tome makes mention of a smoking room, a grill room, a cigar shop, the buffet lounge, the west, east and south rooms as well as private dining rooms and the grand hall, not to mention the Theatre.

What intrigued me about the Alabazam, besides the name, was the use of a whole teaspoon of Angostura. As anyone who regularly uses bitters knows, this is an enormous amount of product for something that is usually measured in drops and dashes, but, tempered with the sugar and Cointreau, it really works in this drink.

Deep red rust in tone and with tons of spice from the Angostura, this cocktail will cure what ails you as you step back in time to an era where drinking was about more than getting blotto'd, it was about following doctor's orders.

> *gaz sez:* Then, the following year, Jamie posted another bitters-heavy cocktail recipe, this one calling for my orange bitters, a fact that he used in order to gig me in the ribs about my age (61 at the time of writing). If the poor boy is lucky enough to survive as long as I, he'll understand that age is a positive thing, not a negative, and I hope that he becomes as happy as I am when he enters his seventh decade here on God's Green

Earth. Here's Jamie's blog posting. First he blathers on about the fine qualities of Partida tequila, then he goes on to say:

It wouldn't be a proper Spirits and Cocktails post without a cocktail, without further ado, I present for your consuming pleasure, the amazing, the splendorific, the marvelous, the incredible, the shocking......

ZIM ZALA BIM

2 oz Partida Reposado

2 bar spoons Regans' orange bitters

2 bar spoons St. Germain Elderflower liqueur

1 bar spoon fine sugar

stir all ingredients to dissolve sugar

add ice and stir

strain into a chilled cocktail glass

squeeze the oil from a lemon peel into glass and

toss the peel

This cocktail was inspired by a recipe that I had found and posted about earlier: the Alabazam. The Alabazam has been getting a lot of play here in Seattle lately, even making the list of my favorite local bar, and I thought that it was high time that I created my own take on this lovely libation, based upon what drew me to the recipe in the first place: a boat-load of bitters.

Just as it is the bar spoon of Angostura that makes the Alabazam, it is the two bar spoons of Regans' orange bitters that makes the Zim Zala Bim. It should be noted that while this drink will work with Angostura orange bitters (it'll just be a completely different beast) it will not work with Fee's orange bitters, so you may as well go out and get yourself a bottle of Regans'. Gary Regan's getting on in years now and any little bit of support we can offer will bring him one step closer to a retirement that is (trust me) loooooong over due (that's right Gary, that was a dig at your age). The spiciness of Regans' orange bitters pairs beautifully with the spicy sweetness of Partida's reposado, and unfortunately Fee's orange bitters are just too simple to do the tequila justice in this case.

St. Germain offers a touch of sweetness to counteract the bitters as well as a beautiful floral note that just makes this drink sing. The sugar is merely there to add a bit of viscosity and to take off any edge that the alcohol may offer.

The Zim Zala Bim is one of those easy concoctions to create that will absolutely wow your guests with its zippy complexity, and as such I have decided that this new creation is an instant Jamie Boudreau classic that I will prepare for years to come, using it to blow away that jaded tequila drinker who is tired of having nothing but margaritas and the million variations that bartenders have created under different nomenclature as their only option for a tequila cocktail.

> ***gaz sez:*** *Not long after his Zim Zala Bim posting, Jamie came up with what might be one of my all-time favorite drinks of his, the Pax Sax Sarax. His excessive use of Peychaud's bitters in this drink makes for a fabulous pairing with the scotch and the Cherry Heering, and he notes, as did* **David Embury***, that licorice (as in Peychaud's) works very well indeed with scotch. Heed Jamie's words, they will stand you in good stead:*
>
> *"Burns Night is rapidly approaching (January 25th) and since we don't really go into the food aspect of bars here on SpiritsandCocktails.com, there won't be any recipes for haggis. What we*

will discuss however, are scotch-based libations, focusing on a recent creation of mine.

"Continuing with our heavily-bittered, magic-worded cocktails of late, I present for you our first concoction, the Pax Sax Sarax. Like the Zim Zala Bim and the Alabazam before it, this is yet another fantastically complex cocktail that uses a boat-load of bitters to good effect.

According to The Complete Book of Spells, Ceremonies and Magic, *the magic phrase Pax Sax Sarax was found in an Elizabethan manuscript in the British Museum, and was purportedly used to prolong orgasm. It was also used to "prevent a person from firing a gun while you are looking into the barrel" according to Albertus Magnus, Being the Approved, Verified, Sympathetic and Natural Egyptian Secrets or White and Black Art for Man and Beast, so as you can see, this is a potent concoction indeed!"*

Call up Penn and Teller so you can dazzle them with the magic behind the:

PAX SAX SARAX

2 oz Glenmorangie single malt

1/4 oz Peychaud's bitters

1/4 oz Cherry Heering

stir all ingredients with ice

rinse cocktail glass with absinthe

strain into a cocktail glass

garnish with 3 brandied cherries

UPDATE: It became apparent today, as I served this libation to guests at my bar, that it is imperative that one not only garnishes this cocktail with the cherries, but that the guest knows that this is part of the experience. The cherries make this cocktail. Ensure that you don't eat them all at the beginning or at the end, but rather space them out throughout the drinking experience.

While these latest concoctions may have a ton of bitters in them, I want to point out that these aren't extremely bitter drinks. The bitters that I have used aren't overly bitter by themselves, especially in the case of Peychaud's which has a pleasant, sweet anise-y finish. One should also keep in mind that I am balancing the bitters with an equal portion of liqueur in both the Zim Zala Bim and the Pax Sax Sarax. The reason why this drink was pretty much a no-brainer for me (the proportions were bang on in its very first incarnation) is as simple as this: licorice and cherry are natural flavour pairings for scotch. The key for this drink was to pick a scotch that was neither too peaty or barrel influenced. Glenmorangie seemed like the obvious, readily available option for this drink, and sure enough it didn't disappoint.

This is a drink for scotch drinkers, and despite the outrageous quantity of Peychaud's bitters present, the scotch still makes its authority known. The bitters, cherry and absinthe flavours all work with the scotch, instead of against, and while I wouldn't suggest this drink to a scotch neophyte, I would probably put it in my top three drinks to give an experienced scotch palate.

> *gaz sez:* To end Jamie's contribution to this year's Manual, *here are a couple more recipes of his that call for outrageous amounts of bitters. The bloody Canadians are uncontrollable, you know.*

Angostura Collins

1 1/2 oz lemon juice

1 1/2 oz simple syrup

shake hard and strain over iced collins glass

layer with 1 1/2 oz angostura

top with 1 1/2 oz soda

straw, lemon twist

Peychaud's Paloma

2 oz grapefruit juice

1 oz tequila

1/4 oz lime juice

1/2 oz simple syrup

shake and strain over iced collins glass

top with 1 oz Peychaud's and 1 oz soda

straw, lime wedge

gaz sez: Before I leave this chapter behind, though, I need to give a nod to Oron Lerner, of the Mapal Bar, Haifa, Israel, who's Old Fashioned No. 6, a drink that calls for a whole ounce of Regans' Orange Bitters, that will be featured in this year's list of 101 Best New Cocktails. Cheers, Oron.

Chapter 14

Ingredient Focus: Extreme Aperol and the No Baloney Negroni

by Camper English

> *gaz sez:* I took Camper's blog on this subject and sort of cut it into pieces a little, then put everything back together in a different order, adding some additional material that Camper was good enough to throw my way. Good chap is Camper.
>
> I do love the way Mr. English relentlessly pursues the odd, and his creation of high-test Aperol, recounted in this essay, is something I never did hear of before. I'm sure that his methodology could be adopted to many weird and wonderful purposes.

Over, now, to Camper English:

As ongoing part of the Solid Liquids Project, I decided to make high-proof Aperol. I haven't talked about this use of dehydrated liqueurs yet, which is making high-proof spirits with them. Simply add neutral grain spirits plus dehydrated liqueur, plus some of the original liqueur to keep taste consistency. First I dehydrated some Aperol.

Dehydrated Aperol

Fill a silicone baking pan or silicone cupcake cups with Aperol liqueur. Place in oven and set on lowest setting (140-170 Fahrenheit, usually). Leave to dehydrate for around 18 hours, squeezing the cup occasionally to break up any top layer of crust that forms, to expose the still-evaporating liquid. The resultant sugar should break up easily (use a muddler or coffee grinder) and be around thirty to forty percent of the starting liquid's volume. Then I made Extreme Aperol.

Extreme Aperol

2 ounces Aperol

2 ounces Everclear Grain Alcohol

1 ounce (by volume) Dehydrated Aperol

Combine ingredients and shake container until dehydrated Aperol is dissolved. (I had to break out the muddler as I had some big chunks.)

Everclear is 75.5 percent alcohol and Aperol is 11 percent alcohol, so by my rough calculations $((.4 \times 75) + (.4 \times 11))$ this comes out to 34.4 percent alcohol. And the stuff is flipping delicious, like Aperol on steroids.

No Baloney Negroni

Then I decided to make a Negroni with it. Many people new to Campari (a Negroni is equal parts Campari, gin, and sweet vermouth) find it too bitter and weird for their taste, so bartenders sometimes substitute the more orangey and less bitter Aperol.

The problem is that Campari is 24 percent alcohol, while Aperol is only 11 percent. I don't think Aperol holds up well in the Negroni. Thus, using Extreme Aperol should keep the same flavor of Aperol but have a higher proof.

To make Extreme Aperol the alcoholic strength as regular Campari I'd need to water it down to 70% Extreme Aperol to 30% water, so in this recipe I just used .75 ounces Aperol instead of the usual ounce.

No Baloney Negroni

.75 ounces Extreme Aperol

1 ounce Gin

1 ounce Sweet Vermouth

Stir all ingredients over ice and strain over new ice in a rocks glass, or strain and serve up if you prefer. Garnish with an orange peel.

Index

Aisha Sharpe 75, 165
Alba Huerta 68
Alex Day 183
Alex Kratena 47
Amanda Boccato 182, 184
Andrew Copsey 140
Anta Lubarte Rosen 78

Camper English 182, 214
Cara Passarelli 80
Cari Hah 84
Carlos Lopez-Flores 44
Carol Donovan 87, 165
Charles Hardwick 165
Charlotte Voisey 69
Cheryl Charming 94
Chris Edwardes 54, 166
Chris Halleron 62
Cris Dehlavi 97

Dale DeGroff 172
Dan Warner 33, 60
Daniel Eun 44
Dave Kaplan 183
David Herpin 31
David Hickling 41
David Wondrich 152
Drake's Drum 52
Dylan Yelenich 64

Ektoras Binikos 157
Elba Girón 21

Emily Chappelle 99
Eric Alperin 44

Felix Crosse 41
Francine Cohen 66
Frank Caiafa 165
franky marshall 120

Gabriella Mlynarczyk 101

Hannah Lanfear 104
Henry Ernest Bryden Besant 150
Hollis Bulleit 68

Ian Krupp 43

Jack McGarry 162
Jamie Boudreau 182, 207
Jared Brown 34
Jeff Grdnich 164
Jenn Tosatto 107
Jeffrey Morgenthaler 165
Jill Saunders 111
Jim Meehan 164
Joann Spiegel 165
Johann Toffa 61
Joseph Albanese 56
Joy Richard 70

Karah Carmack 114
Kitty Amman 70

Laura Lindsay 43
Leo Robitschek 163
Lizzie Asher 68
Lynn House 35, 68, 117
Lynnette Marrero 69

Meaghan Dorman 46, 165
Melanie Asher 68
Michael Butt 144
Michael Joseph Helgeson 23
Michael Neff 18
Michael Parker 57
Murray Stenson 207

Natalie Bovis 48, 124
Nick Strangeway 20
Norman Bukofzer 168

Oron Lerner 37

Pedro Ramirez 48
Philip Duff 73
Philip Greene 177
Philip Ward 164

Raul Dominguez 46
Raul Faria 65
Reinhard Pohorec 24
Richard "Richie" Boccato 182, 183, 194
Robbie Wilson 59
Rosie Schaap 128, 170
Rudi Carraro 47

Sasha Petraske 19
Sean Kenyon 18
Sean Muldoon 162
Sian Ferguson 130
Spyros Patsialos 63
Stan Vadrna 183
Steve Schneider 17

Tad Carducci 164
Tess Posthumus 135
Tim Cooper 20
Tim Judge 39
Tom Macy 147
Tomas Estes 174
Tommie Cheng 19

Whiskey Daisy 67

Yael Amyra 29

About the Author

gaz regan, the bartender formerly known as Gary Regan, works six shifts at The Dead Rabbit in New York City. Every year. He also writes The Cocktailian, a regular column, for *The San Francisco Chronicle*, and he publishes a free e-mail newsletter, *gaz regan's Notion*, that reaches over 10,000 bartenders and consumers by email, and around 20,000 more people on his Facebook pages and via Twitter.

Gaz also maintains the Worldwide Bartender Database, an on-line community that's well over 3,000 strong, and he uses the database to let bartenders know about jobs, competitions, and festivals in *The Weekly Shooter*, a newsletter that goes out every Tuesday, and he also sends solid information to member bartenders on Mondays in a newsletter called *The Bartender Bulletin*. Along with Dushan Zaric and Aisha Sharpe, gaz is one of the founders of The Institute for Mindful Bartending. He has conducted workshops on this subject in Paris, Dubai, Beirut, Moscow, and in various cities in the USA, and he also writes about the subject on his blog, and in his series of books, *The Annual Manual for Bartenders*. "Bartenders can change the world," says gaz, "and mindful bartending can be a good way to start."

www.ingramcontent.com/pod-product-compliance
Lightning Source LLC
Chambersburg PA
CBHW031317160426
43196CB00007B/568